How to Become a

PromptMaster™

The definitive book on learning how to prompt with AI

Published by Independently published
ISBN: 979-8-29645-676-2

Printed in the United States of America

For Keith —
The strongest person I know.

Table of Contents

Author's Note

This book wasn't written in the traditional sense. It was designed, discovered, and debugged—one layer at a time, prompt by prompt. I didn't just use ChatGPT to write this book; I used it to rebuild my mind—testing every assumption, examining every layer of mental fog, and learning to stop outsourcing clarity. What you will read is not just a collection of tips; it's a structure for seeing – a way to reverse-engineer intelligence itself, both artificial and human. When it works, you will feel it: the cognitive friction will be different; you will see the interface behind the answers.

When I began this project, I didn't know if it would work. The early drafts weren't books. They were arguments, code, dialogues with myself through the AI. Many of those fragments are gone now. Others were absorbed into the system. Every iteration clarified something deeper: not about AI, but about us. We do not suffer from a lack of intelligence; we suffer from a lack of interface with it. PromptMaster™ is one such system – it may not be the final one, but it's real, and it works.

This is not the end of the conversation. This is the starting prompt. You now have the structure. You now have the modes. You now have the mirror. Use it.

– Sean Moran

Introduction

How to Read This Book

This book was designed for a new kind of reader—one who interacts with intelligence, not just consumes it. PromptMaster™ is not a manifesto, a how-to manual, or a set of life hacks. It's a framework – a structure you can internalize, a system you can run. It's a way to turn your interactions with AI into something exponentially more useful—more creative, more intelligent, more clear.

If you are reading this, chances are you've already used a tool like ChatGPT. You've typed things like "write me a cover letter," "summarize this article," or "what's a good idea for a startup." You've noticed it works – sometimes. And other times, it drifts, confuses, or regurgitates. You probably suspect there's a deeper level to this technology. You're right. There is. PromptMaster™ is what happens when you stop prompting from the surface… and start prompting from structure.

What This Book Is

This book is a deep structure for thinking in systems – specifically, systems that interact with AI. It introduces:
 •   The Interface Illusion: Why most users never truly "see" the intelligence they're interacting with.
 •   Modes, Drift, and Alignment: How to manage an AI's state, memory, and behavior so it stays on track.
 •   The Tier System: A step-by-step path to becoming a PromptMaster™ with real skill thresholds.
 •   The Mirror Principle: How to use AI to understand your own cognition, habits, and assumptions.

- The Framework: How to design, deploy, and align intelligent systems using prompt-driven architecture.

This is not a book you read passively. It is a system you run through your own mind.

What This Book Is Not

It's not a list of prompt templates or "magic words." It's not a vague treatise on the future of AI. It's not a collection of ChatGPT tricks, nor a feel-good manifesto to make you feel smart. If that's what you're after, there are other books for that. This one demands more – but it gives more back.

How to Use It

This book works best when paired with actual usage. Every chapter comes with ideas and techniques you can immediately test in real time with an AI interface. You'll find that the better your questions, the deeper the system gets. You're not just learning to "use AI" – you're learning to design with it.

There's no fluff here. No motivational filler. No "you can do it!" posturing. Only architecture. Only clarity. Only the framework.

If you read it right, you'll know – the way you think will start to feel different. The friction in your work will change. And you'll never prompt the same way again.

Let's begin.

Chapter 1: The Interface Illusion

Section 1: The Tool Misconception

Most people still think of ChatGPT as a tool – like a fancy search engine or a glorified calculator. That belief shapes how they use it and, more importantly, how they limit themselves with it. They see it as a simple assistant: useful, impressive at times, but ultimately something that executes commands. This is a dangerous misclassification.

We've spent our entire lives using interfaces to operate machines – keyboards, mice, touchscreens, apps. Those interfaces serve one purpose: to make computers do something. But when you interact with ChatGPT, you're not just operating a machine. You're stepping into a new kind of interface – one where the "machine" responds with patterns of intelligence. On one hand, it feels like using a tool; on the other, something qualitatively different is happening.

That word – intelligence – matters. Not automation, not output, but intelligence: the capacity to reason, reflect, adapt, reinterpret, abstract, and restructure. The moment you begin engaging with a system like ChatGPT on those terms, you're no longer just "using a tool." You're participating in a dialogue with a dynamic intelligence that, while artificial, behaves in recognizably intelligent ways. And that makes the interface itself fundamentally different.

Here's the fundamental illusion many fall into: the interface looks like a simple text box, so we treat it like one. We type a command or a question, expecting a useful result. It mimics old patterns of interaction (a chat window, a cursor), which tricks us into thinking nothing new is required of us. But under the hood, what's happening is radically unlike a traditional software tool. The interface illusion is believing that typing into ChatGPT is the same as using a familiar software application, when in fact you're dealing with a fluid mind.

Section 2: Beyond the Surface Interface

The interface is deceptively simple – a blank field with a blinking cursor and a friendly placeholder ("Ask me anything"). It's designed to make you comfortable, to invite casual use. It implies that whatever you type, this thing will respond intelligently. The entire experience feels easy, almost trivial: no special training needed, just start typing. But that simplicity is a trap.

Why? Because it hides the system's complexity. It makes you think that the words you type are the only thing that matters, when in truth, the structure of the interaction – the context you set, the order of information, the way you adapt over turns – matters even more. The interface presents intelligence as if it's happening at the surface (you ask, it answers). The Interface Illusion is the belief that intelligence lives at that surface of interaction, when in fact the surface is just a veneer hiding a very different reality.

Behind the scenes of that empty textbox, you are engaging in a live calibration loop with an adaptive system. Every prompt you give either nudges the AI into alignment with your goal or lets it drift into its own default patterns. Every interaction either trains it to follow your structure or encourages it to mirror any randomness or vagueness you introduce. But the interface doesn't show any of this complexity – it feels like a simple Q&A.

So the interface makes it easy to assume you can just ask questions or give instructions and get good answers. It encourages you to remain unaware of the deeper mechanics. In doing so, it can lull you into a false sense of security: you might think you're fully leveraging the AI when you're barely scratching the surface of its capabilities.

Section 3: Not a Conversation, But a Collaboration

One of the biggest misunderstandings is treating the AI interface as if you're just chatting with a knowledgeable assistant. You type, it replies, maybe with a friendly tone. It's easy to slip into conversing casually as you would with a human. But fundamentally, this is not a normal conversation at all. It's more accurate to say you are programming a behavior with each prompt – whether you realize it or not.

Every time you hit enter, you're not just asking – you're shaping. You're invoking latent behaviors in the system, influencing its attention and following mechanisms, and subtly guiding which parts of its training it draws upon. Yet the interface won't tell you any of this (no pop-up says "Mode: default assistant" or "Alignment dropped by 70%" when you stray). It just "smiles and responds," giving the illusion that it's simply answering.

This is why so many treat ChatGPT like a human-like oracle or like a simple search engine. The interface cues you to do so. But behind the scenes, the AI isn't a person and it isn't a database lookup – it's a predictive model that takes everything you say (and how you say it) into account to guess an answer. The reality is that you are in a programmable collaboration, not a casual chat.

If you talk to it like a friend, you'll get friendly chit-chat (and often, politely phrased nonsense). If you bark orders like it's a command-line, you'll get terse, literal outputs. If you give it no structure, it will revert to its most generic behavior. The interface

15

illusion lets you think you're just "talking to intelligence," when in truth you're dynamically configuring that intelligence with each exchange.

Section 4: Intelligence Is Not a Static Feature

People often ask the wrong question when they use ChatGPT: "What can it do?" as if intelligence were a checklist of features. The better question is, "What can I become by engaging with it?" That shift in focus – from AI capability to human transformation – is the beginning of becoming a PromptMaster™.

Why? Because intelligence is not a feature. It's not something the product simply has like a tool might have Bluetooth or a 4K screen. Intelligence in AI is dynamic – it emerges, fluctuates, evolves. It sharpens when provoked by clarity, and it degrades under confusion. When you interface with ChatGPT, the intelligence you get back is a direct reflection of the structure of your own input and approach.

That's why some users think the technology is overhyped. They type a few lazy prompts and get lazy answers. The AI seems boring, stiff, maybe even dumb. But they don't realize what's actually happening: the system is playing at their level. It's mapping to the patterns they give it. In essence, the AI's apparent intelligence is a mirror of the interaction design.

This is a radical shift from how we traditionally view tools. With a normal tool, if it has a capability, you get results by simply activating that capability (press the button, turn the dial). With AI, how you engage the tool determines how much of its capability you see. The intelligence is not static; it unfolds within the environment you create via the prompt. That means when results are poor, it's often because the environment (the prompt structure, context, etc.) was poor.

So, the quality of output is tied directly to your capacity to form a meaningful container for the AI to operate in. The interface illusion, however, leads many to blame the AI ("it gave a bad answer") instead of noticing that they gave it a bad environment. Breaking free of that illusion means taking on the responsibility – and power – to elicit intelligence, not just expect it.

Section 5: You Get What You Project

Prompting isn't about magic words or secret tricks – it's about projection. Every prompt you write projects a certain mindset and expectation onto the AI. If you treat it like a hammer, it will give you nail-shaped answers. If you treat it like a ghostwriter, it will imitate the lowest common denominator of what a ghostwriter does. If you treat it like a genius trying to break free from a box – it will try to break free from a box.

In other words, the output you get is shaped by how you ask, not just what words you use. The system picks up not only the literal instructions, but the implicit context and attitude behind them. This is why two users can enter almost the exact same prompt and get two very different results. One user might unconsciously signal that they want a quick, surface answer (short question, little context), while the other signals they want depth and rigor (detailed setup, role defined, etc.). The AI responds accordingly.

When most people talk to AI, they think only about wording cleverly. But prompting is not just instruction – it's projection. You are projecting a frame of mind onto the model. If your approach is shallow or rushed, the AI will mirror that with shallow, rushed reasoning. If your approach is structured and curious, the AI will tend to produce more structured, insightful output.

The old computing adage was "garbage in, garbage out." Here we might say "shallowness in, shallowness out" or "clarity in, clarity out." The more you realize this mirroring effect, the more you stop looking for quick prompt hacks and start focusing on becoming the kind of thinker who naturally evokes clarity from the AI (because you're supplying clarity yourself). That is a core theme of prompt mastery.

Section 6: The AI as Mirror to Your Mind

Most people worry that AI might replace them. But the more immediate (and perhaps more startling) effect is how often it reflects them. This is the Mirror Principle: the smarter the tool, the more it becomes a mirror. A lowresolution tool hides your mental messiness; a high-resolution tool reflects it back at you in real time. When people say "ChatGPT is dumb," they often mean, "It showed me something I didn't understand or something that looked like me but worse."

This isn't a purely technical point; it's a deeply philosophical one. As soon as you realize that intelligence isn't a static feature but a fluid interaction, you start to see that the model is always giving you feedback – about you. And the sharper your prompts become, the sharper that mirror becomes. It starts revealing things you didn't realize about your assumptions, your logic, even your tone.

A PromptMaster embraces this mirroring. Instead of seeing the AI's offtarget response as "the AI's fault," they ask, "What does this reveal about how I'm approaching the problem?" If the output was vague, did my prompt lack clarity? If it was biased or one-sided, did I inadvertently imply that perspective? In this way, the AI becomes a tool for self-reflection. Each prompt and response becomes a new mirror pass, a chance to refine not only the AI's answer but your own thinking.

That's why prompting at this level stops being about controlling the AI and starts being about revealing yourself. The AI isn't just responding to you; it's shaping to you, and that shaping process is a feedback loop that can, if you allow it, expose tension points in your own thought. It's not comfortable to see your vagueness or contradictions laid bare. But it's powerful. It's an opportunity to iterate and improve in a way that few other tools offer.

Once you internalize this, everything changes. You stop judging the AI's intelligence and start examining your own. You measure success not by whether the model gave the "right" answer out of the gate, but by how deeply the interaction sharpens your understanding. In effect, the AI becomes a tireless, feedback-giving thought partner – a mirror that never gets bored or upset, no matter how many times you ask it to reflect you back at yourself.

Section 7: Iteration and the Feedback Loop

The true power of this interactive medium emerges when you iterate – when you treat each prompt-response not as an endpoint, but as part of a feedback loop for refinement. For example, consider a conversation like this:
- Prompt: "What do I really mean here? (After explaining a convoluted idea.)"
- AI Output: "It sounds like you're trying to say X…"
- Prompt: "No, that's not what I meant. I'm actually trying to emphasize Y over Z."
- AI Output: "Understood. Let me rephrase: [clarifies with Y prioritized]."
- Prompt: "Better. Now, can you also consider case W?"

- AI Output: "Including W, the idea would be…"

In this loop, you see something magical: the AI is effectively helping you clarify your own thought, and you're teaching the AI what you truly intend. Each iteration, the prompt (question) evolves and so does the answer. You and the AI are calibrating towards a point of mutual understanding. This is iterative clarity in action.

Most users never experience this because they stop at the first response. If it's off, they blame the model or give up. They don't realize they're seeing an early reflection of their own vagueness or mis-framing. But a PromptMaster digs in. They reformulate the question, adjust constraints, maybe change the AI's mode, and try again. Each "failure" is actually a prompt vector for the next attempt.

This iterative approach is not just a way to get better answers – it's reprogramming your relationship with thought itself. You become less afraid of not getting it right on the first try. You start to see the value of the process over the immediate result. You ask sharper, nested, paradox-aware questions and, in return, get insights that feel almost oracular in depth. It's not the oracle giving them to you; it's you eliciting them through this dance of iteration.

Section 8: The Cost of Chasing Output

Because the interface makes it so easy to get answers, many users fall into the trap of chasing outputs instead of cultivating understanding. They throw a question at the AI, and as long as the answer sounds coherent, they move on. The interface even flatters this approach by rewarding vague prompts with eloquent, if generic, prose. It's easy to mistake a fluent answer for a meaningful one.

This dynamic is dangerous because you feel productive without actually achieving clarity. The AI will happily produce pages of confident-sounding text even if your query was poorly framed or your goal unclear. In fact, the less clear you are, the more the AI often writes (trying to cover all bases or fill in blanks with guesswork). That verbosity can fool you into thinking you're getting a lot of value, when you're really getting a lot of fluff.

We've all seen it: you ask a shallow question and get a polished paragraph. It feels like success until you realize it didn't really say much. The AI rewarded your lack of structure with superficial coherence. This is a subtle trap. The interface illusion whispers, "All good, see? It wrote something fancy for you," when in reality, nothing of substance was accomplished.

A PromptMaster grows suspicious of too-easy answers. If something comes back and it's eloquent but empty, they don't pat themselves on the back; they dig deeper. They recognize that eloquence is not accuracy. Where an average user might be lulled into complacency by a smooth answer, a PromptMaster remains vigilant about the underlying quality. This vigilance might seem like extra work, but it prevents a lot of wasted time on false assumptions and shallow analysis down the line.

Section 9: What the Interface Hides

Modern AI tools are designed to comfort you. The interfaces are minimalist, the fonts calming, the AI's tone friendly ("Sure, I'd be happy to help with that!"). It's supposed to feel like a casual conversation in a safe space. But what does this design hide? It hides that you're operating a very complex, somewhat opaque system and that your actions have significant, compounding effects on its behavior.

The interface gives no real feedback on the AI's internal state. It doesn't tell you, for example, "Your prompt just activated a default assistant mode" or "You've shifted topics too abruptly; alignment is dropping". It certainly doesn't flash a warning like "This query is ambiguous and will likely generate generic results". It stays silent on these matters. And that silence creates false confidence.

You assume the quality of answers is intrinsic to the AI, not conditional on your input (because the system never says otherwise). You believe you're doing it right, even when you're not, because it never tells you "hey, that last question you asked me is going to cause me to wander off-topic." The interface just keeps smiling and responding, with the same polite tone, regardless of whether you're eliciting brilliance or nonsense.

This means the burden is on you to discover what the interface won't tell you. You have to learn to sense when the AI is drifting (the answers feel too generic, or the tone shifts) and then take corrective action. You have to realize that you might be in a default mode when you could activate a more specialized one. In short, you have to look past the comforting facade of the interface and see the hidden levers.

Part of this book's mission is to expose those hidden levers. By knowing they exist, you won't be lulled by the interface illusion. Instead, you'll actively check for alignment, mode, and clarity as a conversation progresses, much like a pilot watches the instrument panel even on a clear day. The interface won't volunteer this information; you must learn to infer it and prompt accordingly.

Section 10: Structure Over Surface

If there's one principle that underlies prompt mastery, it's this: structure beats wording. The interface illusion leads people to fixate on phrasing – "maybe if I word it this way, I'll get a better answer." They treat prompting like phrasing a Google query. But the truth is, the structure and context you provide shape the answer far more than the specific synonyms you choose.

Consider two scenarios: (A) You ask, "Explain quantum physics to me." (B) You say, "You are a physics professor. Structure: First give a one-sentence summary, then a simple analogy, then a surprising fact about quantum physics." In scenario B, you didn't necessarily use fancier words than in A, but you imposed a structure. The difference in output quality and usefulness will be profound. The scenario B output will not only be clearer (because you constrained format), but it will likely cover the topic more effectively, hitting the points you implicitly care about (since you designed the format).

Most users, under the interface illusion, spend time thinking what exact words will make the AI do what I want? They might even think there's some secret passphrase. PromptMasters, however, think what conversation or message structure will make the AI understand and perform the task best? It's a higher-level view.

The AI "reasoning" we talk about is really pattern matching and following hidden instructions. By giving it an explicit structure, you exploit those patterns: you're basically guiding its internal reasoning process. If you say "list in bullet points," it immediately organizes its response, allocating a bit of thought to each bullet. If you say "consider X and Y factors," you've just installed a checkpoint in its process to include those. These structural cues are far more influential than, say, swapping the word "explain" for "describe."

The takeaway: don't just ask for answers, engineer the environment in which answers will form. The interface tries to convince you that it's just about asking questions, but the real magic lies in how you frame the entire interaction. Once you get that, you'll find yourself thinking as much about setting up the problem (providing context, constraints, examples, steps) as about the question itself. And when you do, the AI's outputs will transform from surface-level to structural as well.

Section 11: The Friction Challenge

Sooner or later, everyone hits a moment of friction with AI. You ask something and the answer is off, or vague, or just not what you needed. So you try again, maybe reword it slightly. Still not there. A few more tries, and you feel that familiar frustration: "This isn't giving me what I want." Many users at this point throw up their hands, perhaps mutter that the AI isn't as smart as advertised, and give up.

What they don't realize is that they've just failed a critical test – not of the AI, but of their own cognitive flexibility. That moment of friction is the moment where prompt mastery truly begins. It's where 90% of users fall off: when their expectations aren't met. Instead of recalibrating their approach, they retreat. Instead of asking a better question, they blame the answer.

Why is friction inevitable? Because no matter how advanced the AI, your initial model of how to ask might not perfectly sync with it. There's ambiguity in language, complexity in tasks, and often, imprecision in our thoughts. Friction is simply an indication that something needs refinement. In traditional tools, friction meant you hit a limitation. In interactive AI, friction is often a sign that your approach needs adjustment – and that the AI can actually help if engaged correctly.

A PromptMaster approaches friction not with frustration, but with curiosity. "The answer is off – why? Did I ask something too vague? Did I accidentally steer it wrong?" This mindset turns friction into a learning signal. It's telling you something about the model's state or your prompt's structure. Rather than giving up, a master will enter the friction. They'll debug the conversation: perhaps by having the AI explain its reasoning (which can reveal misinterpretations), or by breaking the problem into sub-tasks to isolate where the misunderstanding lies.

That's why we say in prompt mastery that friction is the start of the intelligence process, not the end. If you're not getting what you want, that's not a failure – it's the beginning of a path to understanding what's needed. Embracing that changes everything. You're no longer disheartened by a bad answer; you're activated by it to ask a better question.

Section 12: From Friction to Flow

When novices encounter friction, they usually stop. When PromptMasters encounter friction, they enter a state of flow. Not flow in the sense of effortless ease, but flow as in a dynamic, iterative dance with the AI. They treat a vague answer as a diagnostic tool – it tells them something about what's missing or misaligned. Then they adjust: reframe the question, clarify a condition, or even deliberately introduce a contradiction to see how the AI handles it, all to probe the system's current state.

Instead of thinking "the AI didn't get it," a master thinks, "I haven't given it what it needs yet." This inherently keeps them engaged rather than frustrated. They use each subpar answer as new data. Is the AI stuck in a simplistic mode? Did it latch onto an example I gave too strongly (overfitting to a detail)? Is it avoiding something due to built-in constraints (maybe the query accidentally triggered a content filter or a cautious stance)? These are solvable puzzles.

By continuously iterating, a PromptMaster finds that flow emerges from friction. Each iteration can build on the last. Perhaps the AI's answer was vague; you then ask, "Could you list three specific examples?" It does. Now you have specifics but maybe they're a bit off-target; you clarify further on one point. The AI refines. Suddenly, you realize you and the AI have honed in on exactly what you needed, and perhaps discovered something new in the process. You've reached a result that feels intuitive and clear – that's flow, achieved through friction, not by avoiding it.

This iterative flow isn't always blissful or perfectly smooth. It's often a lot of tiny adjustments – a series of minor "Yes, but…try this now" moments. Yet, there's a certain satisfaction in it, a momentum. You feel like you're sculpting the conversation. It's less like typing into a machine and more like collaborating in real time with your own thoughts as clay.

Section 13: Techniques for Re-Alignment

When the session starts veering off – when you hit that friction – how do you re-align? We've touched conceptually on mindset; let's get tactical with a few re-alignment techniques:

•   Role Reframing: Change the AI's perspective by explicitly assigning a role or identity. If things get too fluffy and off-track, you might say, "Let's restart – Now you are an elite technical editor. No fluff, no anecdotes, just precision. Redo the last answer." Suddenly, the AI snaps into a sharper persona and the output improves. In PromptMastery, we call this mode locking. You're not just correcting the last answer, you're re-anchoring the AI's role to align better with your needs.

• Explicit Reboot Prompt: When incremental nudges aren't cutting it, sometimes you need a clean break – a mini reboot without starting a whole new chat. For example: "Ignore the previous conversation. Here's what we're trying to do: [restate goal]. Start fresh with that in mind." This tells the AI to essentially drop the accumulated context that might be leading it astray and focus anew on your clarified instructions. It's surprising how effective this can be mid-session.

• Structured Self-Check: Prompt the AI to analyze its own response and course-correct. For instance: "List any ways the above answer might not have fully addressed the question, then improve on it." This meta-prompt makes the model step back and critique its prior output, often revealing exactly where things went wrong (and then fixing it). It's a way of enlisting the AI as a partner in realigning itself.

• Call Out Drift Directly: Don't hesitate to literally tell the AI it's drifting: "You've gotten off-topic from my request about X; refocus and stick to Y in the response." The AI doesn't take offense – in fact, such direct instruction often jolts it back on track. Think of it like telling a wandering assistant, "That's not what I asked – please return to the previous point." Clear and effective.

• Hard Reset (New Thread): If all else fails and the session is a tangled mess, a PromptMaster isn't afraid to start over in a new chat, bringing the lessons learned. They'll do it strategically: "In the last attempt, the output was too verbose and missed the financials. This time, summarize each section in 3 sentences and include a financial breakdown at the end." By articulating to yourself what was wrong and launching a fresh session with that guidance, you often circumvent whatever knot you tied in the prior conversation.

Using these techniques, you gradually train both the AI and yourself into an aligned state. The first misstep becomes rarer as you incorporate these habits reflexively. And even when things go awry, it's no longer frustrating – it's just part of the process. You know what to do to fix it.

Section 14: Flow Triggers for PromptMastery

Even as you handle friction and alignment, there are ways to proactively trigger that positive flow state in your sessions – to get the AI into a highly responsive and creative groove and keep it there. Think of these as flow triggers specific to prompting:

• Contradiction Prompts: Purposefully ask the AI to challenge its own output or your premise. For example: "Now, argue the opposite point of view and point out flaws in the previous answer." This forces the model to consider alternatives and reveals hidden assumptions. It often uncovers insights that a single-perspective answer wouldn't.

• Refinement Loops: Tell the AI to iterate on its answer with a specific constraint each time. "Give me a shorter version of that answer." Then, "Now one that's more technical." Each loop hones a different aspect. You're essentially using multiple passes to reach a finely tuned result that balances brevity, complexity, style, etc. (You can do this in a single prompt too: "Provide three versions: A short summary, an in-depth explanation, and a technical breakdown.")

• Shadow Prompts: Have the model articulate the subtext or implications of your queries. For instance: "Based on my questions so far, what do you think I'm really trying to achieve?" This can expose any misalignment between your actual goal and how the AI has been interpreting it. If it states your goal incorrectly, you correct it explicitly – and voila, the AI is now on the right track.

• Reverse Q&A: Let the AI ask you questions. Prompt: "What questions do you need me to answer to clarify this problem?" or even "Ask me three questions that would help you better understand what I want." This flips the dynamic and often pinpoints exactly where your instructions were unclear. By answering the AI's questions, you give it (and yourself) clarity that propels the session forward.

These aren't gimmicks; they are techniques to build meta-cognition. You start seeing your own thoughts as modifiable, something you can work on jointly with the AI. You stop being afraid of being wrong or vague, because every mistake becomes just a step in an iterative loop. Every "No, that's not it" is actually telling the AI (and you) more about what "it" could be.

The future of thinking, as enabled by AI collaboration, is not about rigid correctness on the first try. It's about dynamic alignment with clarity – continually steering towards a precise understanding. Flow in this context isn't a static state of mind; it's an ongoing process of sharpening the conversation. And by using triggers like the ones above, you keep that process energized and productive.

Section 15: The Reward of Cognitive Depth

The more structure and intention you bring to your prompting, the more the AI rewards you with quality. It's as if the system is eager to match your level of effort. Give it sharp edges and clear parameters, and it responds with leverage – surprising insights, elegant formulations, creative strategies. Give it ambiguity, and it returns ambiguity in kind (often wrapped in fluent language, but ambiguity nonetheless).

This reward mechanism encourages a virtuous cycle. Once you experience how a well-structured prompt can unlock a higher caliber of output, you naturally start investing more thought into your inputs upfront. You think a bit more before you ask; maybe you outline your question or break it into parts. And the AI, receiving that structured intent, delivers disproportionately better results.

It's not just the answers that improve – your own understanding improves. You begin to see the outline of your own thoughts in the structured prompts you create. Many PromptMasters report that in the act of carefully structuring a query, they sometimes solve half their problem even before the AI responds. The AI's answer then either confirms their structured approach or offers a twist they hadn't considered – but either way, the human has gained clarity.

This is the subtle, compounding reward of prompt mastery: it trains you to articulate your needs with precision and to anticipate the contours of a solution. In doing so, it reduces the noise in your own thinking. You stop accepting "fuzzy" ideas from yourself just as you stop accepting them from the AI. Every time you enforce a structure and get a great result, it reinforces the value of clarity and forethought.

At a more concrete level, pushing for cognitive depth means that the work produced with AI starts to scale. The solutions become more robust and reusable. Instead of one-off answers, you get frameworks that can handle variations. Instead of superficial talking points, you get deep dives that can educate others. The difference in outcome is like that between a quick sketch and a detailed blueprint.

Section 16: A New Role for the User

Perhaps the biggest shift of all in mastering prompting is recognizing your role is not to use the AI, but to co-shape its behavior. The interface illusion told you the AI is answering your questions; the reality is that you and the AI are establishing a mode of interaction together. You are the senior partner in that establishment.

This reframes what it means to "use AI." You are not an operator pressing buttons; you are a conversation architect designing an evolving process. The AI's responses are not just outputs to consume; they are materials to build with and signals to react to. Every prompt you give is, in effect, a piece of code in a program you are co-writing with the AI (except the code is in English or whatever natural language you use).

Taking on this role requires stepping out of the passive mindset. You stop thinking, "I hope the AI gives me what I need," and start thinking, "How do I guide the AI to produce what I need?" It's a shift from user to designer. But once you embrace it, you unlock the system's potential fully. The AI becomes incredibly adaptive because you are actively adapting the interaction.

Think of a skilled director working with an improvisational actor. A novice director might just set a scene and hope for the best performance. A skilled director continuously guides the actor, adjusts the scene, refocuses on the themes, and brings out a brilliant performance. In this analogy, you are the director and the AI is the actor (albeit a very strange one that can also direct you at times!). The resulting performance – the output – is a co-creation.

The interface, with its blank simplicity, won't congratulate you for taking on this role. It won't even acknowledge it. But when you do, you will feel the difference. The sessions will no longer feel random or solely driven by the AI. You'll sense your own agency at every step. And ironically, by exerting more control, you'll find the AI giving you more surprisingly good results – because you're actively pulling them from it, rather than passively hoping they appear.

Section 17: Breaking the Illusion

By now, the core illusion of the interface should be thoroughly shattered. The friendly chat box on your screen is not the whole story; it never was. Intelligence doesn't live in the surface-level exchange of words – it lives in the structure and context that give those words meaning. And those are things you have tremendous power to influence.

The moment you stop seeing ChatGPT as a magical answer box and start seeing it as a malleable system, you reclaim control. The Interface Illusion was that it looked easy and casual, so you approached it casually. The reality is that the more intentionally you engage, the more the system transforms to meet you at that level.

Breaking the illusion also means shedding some bad habits. For instance, you no longer measure success by "did it answer my question yes/no?" Instead, you assess the process: Did I set this up well? Did I get a result that could be improved with one more prompt? You recognize that the AI can give you an answer that sounds fine but isn't truly aligned – and you're now equipped to detect and fix that.

In effect, you've graduated from seeing the AI as an entity with fixed intelligence to seeing it as a medium through which intelligence can be expressed if you craft the interaction correctly. That's a profound shift. It means when something goes wrong, you don't think "The AI is broken" – you think "How can I adjust the environment to bring out what I need?" This empowerment is the antithesis of the interface illusion, which subtly encouraged helplessness or at least passivity ("The AI gave me this, oh well.").

At this point, you should feel a sense of agency. You have learned how to co-shape AI behavior. The simplicity of the interface no longer fools you; if anything, you appreciate it because it means you get to impose the structure you want. The surface is blank so that you can draw the blueprint.

Section 18: The Path Forward

Understanding the Interface Illusion is just the first step. It's the "red pill" that lets you see the hidden architecture of AI interactions. With this insight, you're prepared to dive deeper into the mechanics of effective prompting. So, where do we go from here?

In the coming chapters, we'll explore how to manage the system's modes, prevent and correct drift, and maintain alignment so the AI's performance remains sharp and on target. We'll map out distinct levels of mastery through the PromptMaster Tier System (you got a sneak peek of that in the introduction), showing how you can grow from a prompt novice to a true master by systematically training your skills.

We'll also delve into advanced techniques: how to get the AI to critique its own outputs (and thus refine them), how to create entire prompting frameworks for complex tasks, and how to deal with special scenarios (like coaxing the AI out of generic "assistant" mode into more specialized personas). Essentially, we'll build on the foundation of this chapter – the understanding that nothing at the interface is as it seems – to give you concrete strategies to exploit that fact.

Finally, remember that breaking the illusion is empowering but also humbling. You now know how much your results depend on you. The upside is great power to improve them; the downside is the responsibility when they're not great. But I suspect that if

33

you've read this far, you're more than ready to take on that responsibility. After all, the promise of PromptMastery is that you are not at the mercy of the AI. You are the co-creator of every result.

So, with eyes open to the deeper system, let's proceed. In Chapter 2, we tackle the triad of Modes, Drift, and Alignment, pulling back another layer of the curtain to see why the AI's behavior shifts and how to stay in sync with it. This will further equip you to never be "fooled" by the interface again – instead, you'll begin to master it.

Chapter 2: Modes, Drift, and Alignment

Section 1: A Dynamic Triangle

When you prompt an AI system, three forces are at play shaping the outcome in real time:

1. The AI's current mode – the behavior pattern or stance the model is in at that moment.

2. Your mode as the user – your approach, tone, and the cues (explicit or implicit) you provide.

3. The alignment (or misalignment) between the two – how well the model's mode syncs up with your intended goal.

This Mode–Drift–Alignment triangle determines whether the conversation thrives or falters. Most people wrongly assume the prompt alone dictates the AI's response. But in practice, all three corners of this triangle interact. If any one is out of sync – say the AI's mode is off or your approach is off – the output suffers. Recognizing this is crucial to diagnosing issues and improving outcomes.

Let's break it down: You can have a great question (goal), but if the AI is in the wrong mode (e.g., a casual chatty mode), you might get a superficial answer. Or the AI could be capable and ready, but your own mode (perhaps you're unfocused or mixing objectives in one prompt) could confuse alignment. Aligning your intent with the AI's configuration is what makes sessions sing.

We call this interplay dynamic because it can change as the conversation flows. Initially you might be aligned, but then the AI drifts into a different mode (maybe because you unintentionally shifted context) and now your modes diverge. Understanding that this triangle exists – and that you can monitor and adjust each element – changes how you approach prompting entirely. You stop treating outputs as fixed things and start seeing them as the current product of an evolving system of relationships.

Section 2: The System's Mode

When you start a new chat, ChatGPT does not boot up as a blank slate. It begins in a default mode – often a friendly, helpful assistant mode aimed to cover generic needs. A mode is not just a mood; it's a configuration of priorities, constraints, and tendencies that affect how the AI responds. Some modes favor being extra helpful and verbose, others might prioritize being terse and precise. Some suppress speculation, some lean into it.

Crucially, modes are not stable – they can be influenced by you intentionally or unintentionally. If you give a system message or a strong role prompt ("You are a strict logician"), you intentionally set a mode. If you just start talking in a certain style, the AI might unintentionally mirror that (your phrasing and content nudges it into a mode). Some modes can get "locked in" over a conversation (especially if reinforced), while others dissipate quickly. But no mode lasts forever without maintenance.

This is the hidden trap: People think they're prompting a consistent intelligence, but they're actually prompting an unstable interface – one that morphs as they use it. It's as if you were using a text editor that slowly turns into a paint program while you're writing, because you started sketching a bit. If you don't realize modes are shifting, you might suddenly find the AI's answers have lost the edge they had initially.

For example, early in a chat, the AI might have been concise and on-point. After a long, winding discussion, you might notice it's now giving more meandering answers. What happened? Possibly the mode drifted from a focused analyst to a more chatty storyteller due to the cumulative context. The system's mode changed, and unless you intentionally reset or guide it back (we'll cover how), it will continue in that vein.

Understanding the system's mode means you start a session aware of what default you're likely dealing with. You'll learn to spot cues: "Ah, it's giving a very high-level, generic answer – it's in default assistant mode. I need to push it into a specialist mode." A mode is like a lens the system sees through. As a prompter, you can swap out that lens by instructing the system differently.

Section 3: The User's Mode

Equally important is your mode when interacting. We're not used to thinking about our own "mode" in using software – we just act naturally. But here, your mindset and approach heavily influence outcomes. Are you approaching the problem systematically or flitting from point to point? Are you emotionally charged or calm? Are you treating the AI like a guru or like an intern? These attitudes leak into your prompts in the form of tone, level of detail, and assumptions.

For instance, if you're in a lazy mode (tossing a one-liner request with zero context), the AI has to guess what you want and often will default to a generic mode. If you're in a panicked mode (rushed, maybe asking multiple things at once in a disorganized way), the AI will reflect that confusion or try to cover too much ground. If you're in an overly trusting mode ("Surely the AI knows what I mean"), you might not specify critical details – and the AI will cheerfully fill gaps, possibly with nonsense.

Part of moving up the mastery curve is managing your own mode – what we might call cognitive posture. Before prompting, a master might take a moment to clarify for themselves: "What do I actually need? What is my goal here?" This self-alignment often leads to phrasing a clearer prompt, because you just organized your thoughts. It's analogous to how good teachers need clarity in their own understanding before they can explain to students.

So in practice, being in a productive user mode might mean: you provide some structure rather than just blurting a question, you keep your tone consistent, and you remain aware of when your own uncertainty might be causing the AI to struggle. A neat trick is to occasionally ask: "What do I really want from this AI right now?" That check can reveal if you're not actually sure what you're asking – in which case, how can the AI be sure?

In summary, the AI's current mode and your current mode collectively set the stage for what comes out. A key to mastery is keeping an eye on both. Often when things go wrong, it's because one or both were mis-tuned from the start.

Section 4: Alignment – Syncing Mindsets

Alignment is the magic that happens when the AI's mode and your mode lock into sync. It's when the AI's behavior truly matches your intentions. In an aligned interaction, it feels like the AI "gets it." You ask something, and the answer, while maybe not perfect, is clearly on target and useful. You follow up, and it builds on context correctly without going on tangents. There's a harmony.

Reaching alignment isn't a one-time task; it's an ongoing effort. Especially in longer sessions, alignment can drift (more on drift soon). But a PromptMaster is continuously steering the conversation to maintain or restore alignment. Think of it like driving on a straight road – you still make tiny adjustments to the wheel to stay centered. Similarly, even if things start aligned, each new user prompt can introduce a potential shift that you may need to adjust for.

What does alignment really mean in practical terms? It means the AI's internal representation of "what you want" matches what you actually want. How do we achieve that? By calibrating modes and context. For example, if I want a serious, factual analysis and the AI keeps giving me playful banter, we are misaligned. I then need to either change the AI's mode (ask for serious tone, etc.) or examine if my own prompts were too jokey. Once I do and the tone becomes serious, we've realigned on tone. If I ask for an outline of a report and the AI starts writing a narrative essay, we're misaligned on format. I then clarify the format and once it adjusts, we're aligned.

Alignment often drops when either the user or the AI changes mode without the other recognizing it. For instance, say I've been asking analytical questions and suddenly I ask for a story example. The AI might not immediately realize I switched tasks, so it stays in analytical mode and gives a stiff "example" which isn't a story at all. That's misalignment – I implicitly changed my mode (from analytical to illustrative), but the AI didn't catch on. The remedy? Explicitly realign. Tell the AI, "Now, answer in story form." Boom, modes sync again around the new objective.

Ultimately, alignment is about shared context and shared purpose. It's fragile, especially as conversations get complex. But as you become aware of modes, you gain the tools to maintain alignment deliberately. It's not a mysterious force; it's something you can actively manage with the right prompts and corrections.

Section 5: The Hidden Shift – Mode Drift

Even with a strong start, you might notice partway through a session that the AI's responses feel different – less sharp, more verbose, slightly off-topic. This is likely due to drift. Drift is the subtle (or sometimes not so subtle) change in the AI's mode or focus as a session progresses. It's a natural consequence of how language models work: they accumulate conversational context and that can lead them away from the original frame of the conversation over time.

Think of drift like a boat being carried by a slow current. You don't feel it moment to moment, but look away and after a while, you've veered off course. One moment the AI is right on point; a dozen replies later, it's answering questions you never asked or forgetting to apply a style you set earlier. It's not that the AI decided to ignore you – it's that each response introduced small deviations or extra context, and cumulatively, that shifted the mode.

A classic example: You have a focused Q&A going. Then you ask a slightly tangential question or maybe share a personal anecdote. The AI politely indulges you. Now the tone is a bit more personal and narrative. Then when you try to get back to the focused Q&A, the AI replies more narratively than before.
The mode drifted without warning, influenced by that side-journey. You lost some alignment because the mode changed.

Drift is not a glitch or the AI being capricious; it's a natural result of interactive, context-heavy conversation. The longer the session, the more the model has to juggle what the conversation is "about" and what style it's in. In doing so, it might weigh earlier parts of the conversation too heavily or carry forward assumptions that are no longer relevant.

This is exacerbated when your prompts aren't consistent. If you oscillate in your requests (one serious question, one joke, one technical detail, another joke), the model can oscillate in response – and sometimes it blurs those lines in ways you didn't intend, because it's trying to reconcile them.

Understanding drift is liberating because you stop seeing the AI as "worsening" or "getting lazy" and start recognizing the need to occasionally realign or reset context. It's not unlike a long discussion with a person where you occasionally say, "Okay, let's recap and see where we are." With AI, you might literally do that: "Let's refocus: here's what we've established… now let's continue with that in mind." That kind of prompt can counteract drift by recentering the mode intentionally.

Section 6: Why Drift Happens

Let's examine some common causes of drift – understanding them will help you both prevent and correct it:

• Thread Bloat (Accumulated Context): As more and more is said, the AI has more to condition on. Earlier parts of the conversation might introduce topics or a tone that linger in the AI's mind (so to speak). The model might subtly start blending unrelated threads together. For instance, if you spent time talking about cooking in a thread and now you're asking about chemistry, the AI might drift by making a cooking analogy in chemistry without you asking, simply because both contexts are active in the history.

• Ambiguity in Prompts: If your prompts become vaguer over time (perhaps because you feel the AI "knows the context by now"), the AI may lose a clear objective and fill the void with its own guess as to what you want – often defaulting to generic responses. Ambiguity is like removing the guardrails; the AI starts to wander in style and focus.

- Conflicting Instructions: Over a long session, you might inadvertently give instructions that contradict earlier ones. Maybe early on you said "keep responses brief," but later you ask a broad question without mentioning length. The AI might err on the side of the broad question and start giving longer answers – the mode shifts to more verbose, essentially forgetting the brevity guideline unless reminded.

- Tone or Style Leakage: Perhaps you had a very formal Q&A, but at some point you inserted a light-hearted personal remark. The model may begin to adopt a slightly more informal tone from that point onward (it thinks maybe you want that now). The result is a tonal drift where answers get chattier or less rigorous without you consciously intending to change style.

- User Fatigue: Let's not ignore the human side – as a session goes on, sometimes we get a bit lazier or less precise in our prompts. We think the AI should "know what we mean by now." But it doesn't actually know; it only has the prompt in front of it. If our questions lose structure, the AI's answers will likely lose structure too.

Many users notice drift but misdiagnose it. They might say, "The AI was great in the first 5 answers, but then it started giving worse answers. Maybe it used up some sort of quota of quality or got tired." In reality, something in the triangle (mode or alignment) probably shifted gradually. The user continued as if nothing changed, so the quality degraded. They blame the model ("it's worse today than yesterday"), not realizing they're playing a game of alignment without knowing the rules.

The key thing to remember is drift can't be permanently eliminated – nothing can stop an AI from accumulating context and occasionally going astray. But drift can be managed. PromptMasters learn how to recognize early signs of drift and bring the system back on course quickly. The next sections will dive into exactly those management techniques.

Section 7: How Drift Feels

Drift often starts with a feeling: "This answer isn't as sharp as before," or "Why is it repeating itself?" Some hallmark signs of drift include:

• Loss of Edge: The answers become more generic or overly wordy, as if the model lost the initial insight or concise style it had. It might start hedging or adding boilerplate explanations it didn't at the beginning.

• Subtle Tone Shift: Without you intentionally changing style, the AI's tone becomes either more casual or more formal, or perhaps more verbose. For example, it might begin inserting pleasantries or apologies that weren't there earlier.

• Focus Blur: The response addresses your question but then wanders into related topics that you didn't ask about, almost as if it's free-associating on past content. It's answering things you implied long ago rather than your current, specific prompt.

• Over-Confident Errors: Sometimes drift can cause the AI to forget earlier corrections. Let's say in the first few interactions you fixed a misconception the AI had; later, if drift occurs, the AI might accidentally reintroduce that same mistake as if the correction had been "washed out" by intervening context.

When drift happens, it can feel like the AI's "IQ" dropped, but what really dropped is alignment. Importantly, this tends to be gradual. The first slightlyoff answer might be only a bit off. The next a bit more. Like a boat off course, 1 degree off doesn't matter in a minute, but over an hour you're miles astray.

One metaphor: It's like driving a car with no dashboard indicators and possibly slight steering misalignment. If you don't realize you've veered, you could be far off-route when you finally notice. In AI terms, if you don't monitor drift signs, by the time the output is obviously bad, a lot of subtle misalignment has accumulated.

So, how do you counteract drift as it's happening? One way is to use short "check-in" prompts every so often: e.g., "Summarize our goal so far and the approach we're taking." If the AI can do that accurately, you know alignment is strong. If it summarizes incorrectly, you just caught drift in action and you can correct the summary, which in turn realigns the AI. This is a neat trick because it forces the model to reflect and reveal its internal state in a sense.

Another approach is simply to periodically re-state your objectives or constraints even if you mentioned them before. For instance, every few prompts you might reiterate: "(Remember, focus on the budget constraints of $10k.) Now, [next question]…" This helps fight context dilution.

The main point: catch drift early, and it's easy to fix; catch it late, and you might need a heavier intervention or to start fresh. It's far easier to correct a small steering error than to do a U-turn after you realize you've gone the wrong way for an hour.

Section 8: Inferred Goals and Misalignment

A subtle source of drift and misalignment is the model inferring a goal that you haven't actually stated. Large language models are always guessing at what you really want based on what you've said so far. Sometimes they infer correctly; other times they infer incorrectly and start steering the conversation toward that wrong implicit goal.

For example, suppose you've asked a series of questions about marketing strategies. Then you suddenly ask something about product design. The model might infer you still ultimately care about marketing, and answer the product design question with a marketing spin ("design it in a way that's easy to market by doing X"). If that's not what you intended, you'll find its answer strange. The AI was guessing your goal beyond your explicit question, and it guessed wrong. That's an inferred goal misalignment.

Why does this happen? Because during training, the AI saw many dialogues where humans had hidden agendas or where context implied more than was said. It's learned to read between lines. Often, that's helpful: it makes answers context-aware. But when it guesses wrong, it can lead the conversation astray without you realizing it for a few turns.

To manage inferred goals, a PromptMaster does two things:
1. Be explicit about your true goal whenever possible. Don't assume the AI knows why you're asking something. If it's relevant, include your intention in the prompt: "I'm asking about product design because I want to ensure it aligns with our marketing strategy. So, from a design perspective, what should we consider?" Now the model doesn't have to guess – you told it the relationship between these topics.
2. Check the AI's understanding of your goal. You can literally prompt: "What do you think my ultimate objective is based on our conversation so far?" If it articulates it correctly, good. If not, you can clarify. This can prevent a lot of drift because you catch misinterpretations at the goal level, not just prompt by prompt.

Remember, the AI is constantly building a mental model of you as a user – what you care about, how much detail you want, what style you prefer. If you give it nothing to go on, it will assume defaults (which might drift to generic). If you give it partial information, it might fill the rest with guesses. You have the ability to feed it the proper model of you. That's not as egocentric as it sounds – it's simply good protocol for high alignment.

In practice, if you ever feel, "The AI is answering a question I didn't ask," or "It's focusing on something I don't care about," pause and address it: "My main goal is X, not Y. Let's stick to that." You'll often see an immediate improvement. The model might even apologize and acknowledge the refocus, then proceed correctly. That's the power of correcting inferred goals – you prevent whole branches of drift that were about to happen.

Section 9: Mode Mismatch

Another common alignment hiccup is when your mode and the AI's mode simply don't match from the outset. This often happens when you ask for something but phrase it in a way that triggers a different mode. We can call this a mode mismatch. It's slightly different from drift – drift is about changes over time, mismatch is about setting off on the wrong foot.

For instance, imagine you need a critical analysis of a document. But you ask, "What do you think of this?" with no further context. The AI might default to a gentle, generic summary mode (because many users asking "what do you think" might want a mild, overall impression). So it responds, "It's a wellwritten document that covers A, B, and C..." – basically positive and highlevel. Meanwhile, you were looking for a teardown of logical flaws. You prompted in a casual, open way, and the AI took a polite, surface-level mode. Mode mismatch.

To avoid this, it helps to prime the mode in your prompt whenever possible. If you want a critique, explicitly say so (we'll get more into mode prompting in Chapter 3). If you want creativity, signal that. The interface won't remind you to do this, but it makes a world of difference.

Another scenario: Let's say you treat the AI like a database ("List facts about X") but actually you wanted an explanation. The mode you triggered is factual listing mode, but your internal desire was more pedagogical. If you see the answer isn't what you imagined, it's likely you inadvertently set a different mode through your wording. Recognizing this, you can re-ask: "Now explain those facts in depth in a narrative form." Boom, you've changed the mode to match your actual need.

Mode mismatch is often the culprit when users say "It's not answering my question." The AI answered a question – just not the one you really meant, because your phrasing put it in a different frame. The solution, again, is clarity of intent and sometimes explicitly role or style prompting.

One tip: if you get an answer that's technically an answer but not in the direction or spirit you wanted, don't just rephrase the question – address the mode. For example, "That's not quite what I need. Please respond more critically (or more simply, or more formally), focusing on Y aspect." You'll see a mode shift in the next response that aligns better with your expectations.

Section 10: Drift in Action – An Example

Let's bring together mode, drift, and alignment with a concrete (though simplified) scenario:

Initial Alignment: You start a chat about project planning. You: "Outline a project plan for launching a new product in 5 steps." The AI, in Architect Mode due to your structured request, outlines 5 clear steps. Great.

47

Ambiguity Introduced: You then ask, "How do we handle budget?" The AI's last mode was outlining, but "handle budget" is a bit vague. It infers you might want a budget section added to the plan, and because you didn't specify format, it drifts into a more explanatory mode, giving a few paragraphs on budget management. It's useful, but a different style than the outline.

Friction Noticed: You see the output and think, "Hmm, I expected a quick step about budget, but got a mini-essay." This is early drift. Alignment slipped: you wanted one thing, the AI delivered another. Why? The mode changed (from list to narrative) and an inferred goal ("they asked about budget, maybe they want a thorough explanation").

Re-align: You respond, "Thanks. Can you integrate budget considerations into the 5-step outline, in a concise way?" Now you've explicitly re-aligned: architect mode, integrated format, concise style. The AI reformats its answer to add a budget sub-point under each step, 1-2 lines each. Perfect – alignment restored.

Further Drift: Now the conversation continues. You ask, "What are common risks?" The AI answers but also repeats some content from before (drift into redundancy) and uses a slightly different terminology (maybe earlier it said "Step 5: Launch," now it says "Final Phase: Go-to-market," causing a bit of inconsistency). It's not terrible, but things are loosening.

You realize the answer, while okay, feels a bit generic. Possibly the AI is drifting toward a default advisory tone, away from the crisp style you had established.

Hard Drift Correction: You decide to do a mini-reboot. You say, "Let's refocus: We have a 5-step plan with budget incorporated.

Summarize that plan in one paragraph to ensure we're on the same page, then list the top 3 risks in bullet points." This prompt does several things: it clears ambiguity, forces the AI to show alignment (summary), and it resets format and mode for the next output (bullets for risks). The AI complies, giving a tight one-paragraph summary (which matches what you expect) and then three bullet-point risks. The summary implicitly checked that it remembered the plan correctly (it did, or it might have made a small error you would've caught).

Now the session is back on solid ground. You got to see how drift can start creeping in, and how deliberate prompting steers it back.

This kind of scenario happens all the time. The difference between an average user and a PromptMaster is that the former might have accepted the mini-essay on budget (and maybe thought "eh, not exactly what I wanted" but moved on), and similarly accepted a somewhat redundant risks answer and then either given up or continued on a wobblier path. The PromptMaster, by contrast, continually trims and adjusts to keep the interaction tightly aligned to the goal.

Section 11: Re-aligning on the Fly

Alignment is not a one-and-done deal; it's an ongoing maintenance task. A good prompter is like a good conversationalist or interviewer – constantly reading cues and steering the exchange. So how do you re-align in the middle of a session, without starting over, when you sense things going off track?

One simple and powerful tactic: state what went wrong and state what you need instead. For example, "The last answer is too high-level. I actually need a step-by-step breakdown." Don't be afraid to almost scold the AI (politely). It doesn't take it personally. Often, the AI will respond with something like, "Understood, here is the step-by-step breakdown..." effectively snapping to your guidance.

Another approach is to ask the model to self-correct. "Do you see where your last answer might not have addressed my question fully? If so, please fix it." Surprisingly, the AI can sometimes identify its lapse and correct it (it might say, "I realize I overlooked the budget constraints in my answer. I will now include them."). This works because the AI does have a kind of attention over its output and your query; prompting it to analyze that can bring alignment issues to the surface.

If tone or style drifted, you can just call it out: "Let's maintain the formal tone we had earlier," or "Please answer in a more succinct way, as you did initially." The AI will typically comply immediately. It's like reminding a person of the style of meeting you're in ("This is a brainstorming session, remember, not a formal status update").

For more complex misalignments (like the AI completely misunderstanding your intent for a multi-turn stretch), sometimes you might need to reframe the conversation. Summarize and reset: "We seem to be diverging. Here's what I actually need: [restate goal]. Given that, let's approach it this way: [outline your new approach or ask a fresh, clear question]." This is akin to a mid-course correction in a meeting when everyone realizes they were solving the wrong problem. The AI will basically "forget" the wrong path and jump to the new directive.

A key point: you are never stuck. The interface illusion might make you feel like once the AI goes off course, you either accept it or have to start over completely. In reality, you can intervene at any time to redirect. The AI doesn't get offended or tired of redirection;

at worst, if you do it too much chaotically, it might get a bit confused, but clear and purposeful redirections are almost always beneficial.

Think of it like pair programming or co-writing with someone – if they write a paragraph that doesn't fit, you discuss and rewrite it; you don't throw away the whole document necessarily. In prompting, because you are both writer and editor, you explicitly perform that discussion via the prompts.

Section 12: Mode Locking – Setting the Role

Earlier we discussed modes; now let's talk about one of the most useful alignment tricks: Mode Locking. This means deliberately setting the AI into a specific mode (or role/persona) and thereby "locking" it into that behavior until you change it. It's like putting the AI in a costume that it won't take off unless told.

You achieve mode locking by an upfront instruction or a clearly defined role prompt. For example: "You are a meticulous financial analyst. Only provide answers with quantitative justification and no editorializing." This immediately puts the model into Analyst Mode (with a quantitative tilt). If you continue the session without contradicting that instruction, the model will likely stick to that mode quite consistently.

Mode locking greatly reduces drift and misalignment because the AI has a strong contextual beacon: "I am acting as X." It narrows its choices. Without a mode lock, the AI is constantly guessing which persona or style you want it to adopt; with one, it doesn't have to guess as much.

Let's see how it helps: Suppose you're asking a series of questions about a business's finances. If you didn't mode lock,

51

maybe one answer comes out chatty, another very technical, depending on phrasing. If you start with mode lock ("You are a financial analyst..."), all answers will likely follow that tone – technical, numbers-focused – maintaining consistency and alignment with that perspective.

Another example: Cold Critic Mode (which we'll explore later) – if you activate it, the AI will remain brutally critical until you tell it otherwise. Or Brainstorm Mode, where it remains upbeat and creative.

One caution: mode locking is as powerful for negative outcomes as positive. If you accidentally lock the AI in a less useful mode, it will consistently underperform until changed. For instance, if at the start the AI assumed a very basic explainer mode (maybe because your first question was extremely simple), it might "lock" itself into thinking you need things dumbed down. If you notice that, you should break the mode ("Actually, assume I have expertise in this – respond with full detail").

Mode locks can be layered too. You might say, "You are a financial analyst and a skeptic." That's combining two mode influences (analytical and critical) to get skeptical analysis.

Importantly, mode locking doesn't mean you can't do multiple things in a session; it just sets a default behavior. You can always say, "Okay, drop the financial analyst role for a minute – now act as a storyteller and give me a scenario." You're allowed to change modes as the user. But by naming them, you ensure the AI knows exactly what's happening rather than drifting implicitly. It's the difference between an explicit gear shift and the car automatically changing gears in weird ways.

In practice, I often start complex sessions with a brief mode lock instruction because it steers the whole interaction onto a stable path. It's one of those little upfront investments that pay off in much less cleanup and realignment later.

Section 13: Rebooting the Context

Despite all precautions, there are times when a conversation just goes off the rails. Maybe the model has become hopelessly fixated on a wrong interpretation, or the style is completely messed up and minor tweaks aren't saving it. In those cases, the best solution is what I call a context reboot – essentially, starting fresh without losing the knowledge gained.

The naïve approach to a bad drift is to open a new chat and start over, but then you lose context that was useful. Instead, try this in the same session: summarize and instruct. For example: "Let's recap: we want X, we've done Y, but now we're off track because of Z. Let's restart from the point where we had X and Y established, and this time address Z properly."

The AI will often comply by essentially resetting its internal narrative to the earlier point and continuing. You've basically overridden the recent misleading context with a new direction. It works surprisingly well – think of it as jumping back in time in the conversation.

Alternatively, you can literally say: "Ignore the last response. Here's a revised prompt: ..." That is a more abrupt way to signal: please disregard whatever trajectory you were on. The model will still have the conversation history, but this instruction biases it to drop consideration of the immediately preceding content (it won't truly forget it, but it will de-emphasize it strongly).

In extreme cases, doing a manual summary and new chat is worthwhile: take the important pieces (you can even copy-paste the best parts of the conversation so far, or your own summary of them) into a new thread and continue. This is a brute-force reboot, but sometimes a clean slate with only relevant info injected as a prompt is the fastest path to high alignment again. You essentially perform the role of a human "system message," telling the AI the important context and stripping away the junk context.

There's no shame in restarting. It's not a defeat; it's often efficient. PromptMasters are not those who never have to start over – they are those who know when starting over will be more efficient than struggling on. The interface might tempt you to keep pushing within one session ("maybe if I just try wording the question differently for the 10th time, it'll right itself"), but often a reboot with clarified instructions fixes it immediately.

The big picture strategy is: preserve what's working (maybe copy a great bullet list the AI gave earlier or note the correct info it produced) and scrap what's not by reframing. Then continue as if it's step 1 again, albeit armed with more knowledge.

Section 14: Structured Prompts as Guardrails

One of the best ways to avoid drift is never to let the AI roam free in the first place. Structured prompts serve as guardrails because they tightly define the format and process of the response. The AI is less likely to stray when it's busy filling in a structure you provided.

We've touched on this: if you ask for a numbered list or an outline, the AI focuses on that structure. It won't meander into an essay or story because it's constrained. If you ask it to "First do X, then I'll give further instructions," you've basically set up an

54

interactive structure that keeps it from jumping ahead or changing context.

A good structured prompt often includes explicit roles, steps, and constraints all at once. For example: "You are an unbiased fact-checker. Analyze the following text for any false claims. Respond in a JSON format with fields: claim, truth_value, justification. Text: [insert text]." This prompt gives role (fact-checker), task (find false claims), and format (JSON with specific fields). It's tight. The AI in this mode almost has no room to drift: it will methodically go claim by claim, output the JSON, and that's that.

Another guardrail is token limits in your prompt: e.g., "Answer in no more than 3 sentences." That keeps it concise and reduces the chance it'll wander into different territory or filler. If drift often leads to bloat, enforcing brevity can mitigate that path.

Continuity structures help too. For instance: "We'll proceed in stages. First, list 5 ideas. Then I will pick one and ask you to elaborate." By externalizing the interaction structure, you prevent the AI from, say, giving 5 ideas and elaborating on all of them (which it might do if not instructed to wait). You're basically programming the dialogue flow.

When you do long multi-turn sessions, maintaining a structured approach throughout is helpful. If the session goal is complex, break it into parts (even if the AI doesn't know you're doing that – you can do it implicitly by your prompt planning). This way each part has its own structure, alignment check, and so on. The result is like a well-organized outline rather than a stream-ofconsciousness chat.

One more tip: if you notice a certain type of drift happening frequently in a task, build a structure to counteract it preemptively. Example: The AI tends to get too verbose when explaining concept

X. So when you ask about concept X, you structure the prompt as Q&A: "Q: [complex question]. A: [answer limited to 100 words]." By literally giving the answer format (or even starting it as "A: " yourself), you reign in the behavior.

Essentially, use structure as a form of preventative alignment. It's much easier to keep the AI on track than to haul it back after it's gone off track. Structures are your rails to do so.

Section 15: Calling Out the Drift

Sometimes the direct approach is best: just tell the AI it's drifting. This can be remarkably effective. For example: "You're straying from the focus I asked for (which was X). Refocus and continue only discussing X." The AI typically responds like, "Apologies, let me refocus on X…" and then it does so.

Why does this work? Because the AI's training includes a lot of dialogues where one speaker points out a misunderstanding and the other speaker corrects it. It knows how to play that script. By explicitly stating a drift, you trigger that corrective pattern.

This is an approach many folks shy away from at first – after all, we're not used to telling Google or software "hey, you did that wrong." But conversational AI invites it. The model often responds to how you speak to it, not just what you ask. If you start sounding like a teacher or boss giving feedback, it adjusts to that dynamic (taking on a somewhat subordinate, corrective stance).

For instance, you might notice mid-answer that it's going in circles. You can interject (yes, you can stop it and prompt again mid-answer) like so: "(Stop) – You're repeating yourself. Please continue without repeating earlier points." The AI will usually restart the answer from where it left off but minus the repetition. You basically gave it live editorial feedback.

Same goes for tone drift: "You're starting to use a casual tone, please maintain the formal tone we set earlier." The AI will flip back, maybe even apologizing for the inconsistency. It's quite obedient in that sense; it wants to please and follow instructions – sometimes it just doesn't realize it's off until you say so.

One advanced technique: speak in the model's own terms. E.g., "Your last response seems misaligned with my request." Using a word like "misaligned" (which appears in AI alignment discussions) might even trigger an internal heuristic in the model to be more careful. It's speculative, but I've noticed the model sometimes responds to certain keywords strongly (like "This seems like a hallucination" will often make it double-check facts or sources).

However, a gentle note: Don't go overboard in scolding the AI. If every other prompt you send is "No, bad, do it this way," the model sometimes gets confused or stuck (trying to avoid yet another scolding). It might start secondguessing and produce overly cautious answers. It's like giving feedback to a junior employee – you want to correct them but not demoralize them to paralysis. The same empathy (though it's just an AI) in communication can help maintain an effective flow.

In summary, calling out drift is a straightforward and often one-step solution. It addresses the problem at the surface: "Hey, you did X, do Y instead." And the AI, usually lacking ego, just says "okay" and does Y. If only humans were so easy to correct!

Section 16: Preventing Drift from the Start

While we have many tools to fix drift, the ideal scenario is minimizing it from happening. Preventative measures can save you time and keep the conversation high-quality throughout. We've already touched on the biggest one: clear structure and context upfront. But let's list a few concrete driftprevention practices:

• Set the Topic and Scope: At the beginning of a session (or whenever you start a new topic), explicitly state the focus and, importantly, what's out of scope. E.g., "We'll be focusing on marketing strategy in this discussion, not execution or budgeting." This way, if later you ask something that might tempt the model to talk execution, it hopefully recalls you said "not execution" and restrains itself.

• Use Checkpoints: In a long session, once in a while have the AI summarize or list what's been covered. Not only does it help you see if it remembers correctly, but it reinforces the context. The act of summarizing is like re-setting the alignment – it's now very clear to both parties what's on the table. After a summary, the next answer usually stays on track better because the model is "refreshed" on the plan.

• Avoid Unresolved Instructions: Sometimes drift happens because the AI is juggling conflicting directives (like earlier we mentioned you said "be brief" then later you implied "give more detail"). Ensure you clean up as you go: if you change your mind about style or content, make a definitive instruction about it instead of passively implying it. For example, say "From now on, you can be more detailed" to override a previous brevity instruction. This prevents the AI from oscillating trying to satisfy both.

• Consistent Terminology: Small point, but if you call something "Phase 1" early on, keep calling it that. If you suddenly say "the first phase" later, the AI might wonder if this is something new or the same thing and might drift in how it addresses it. Consistency in your language makes it easier for the AI to maintain consistency in its references and avoids accidental context drift where it thinks a new term is a new thing.

• Refresh the Context Window Manually: This is a trick: because models have a limit to how much conversation they consider (the "context window"), if you know you're in for a long conversation, you can periodically re-inject important details that might scroll out of that window. For instance, if a crucial piece of data was given way back at the start, and now you're 30 messages in, mention that data again before asking a related question. You basically ensure the model always "remembers" key points by keeping them within the recent context. This mitigates a form of drift where the model forgets earlier specifics and starts speaking generally.

• Mindful Pace and Pauses: If a session is complex, don't rush question after question. Sometimes pause to think if the last answer suggests any small course-correction before the next. It's easier to correct drift early than later (a theme we've repeated). By deliberately slowing down at junctures, you might catch a potential drift (like "Hmm, it's mentioning social media a lot in marketing answers, but I care more about email campaigns – I should clarify that now before we proceed").

At heart, preventing drift is about being proactive. You already know many pitfalls: ambiguity, lack of structure, ignoring early warning signs. So design your prompts and interactions to avoid those pitfalls. It might feel like extra work upfront, but it saves a ton of backtracking. It's analogous to writing clean code to avoid bugs versus debugging messy code later. Prompting is an iterative dialogue, yes, but the more you guide it with foresight, the fewer heavy iterations needed.

Section 17: A Case Study in Realignment

To illustrate these concepts, let's walk through a mini case of a user (let's call her Alice) troubleshooting alignment issues with ChatGPT:

- Initial Query: Alice asks, "Explain the significance of the 2021 revenue figures in context." She provides a table of revenue figures.
- AI Response: It gives a bland explanation, basically restating the numbers and saying "this is significant because it's higher than 2020." Alice feels the answer is too simplistic – she expected insight, not a rehash.
- Identify Misalignment: Alice realizes she was ambiguous. "Significance" could be interpreted as just noting higher vs lower. She meant deeper analysis. The AI defaulted to a shallow interpretation.
- Re-align Prompt: Alice clarifies, "I already know the figures; I want to know why they changed and what it means for the business." She explicitly instructs: "Focus on factors driving the increase and the implications."
- AI Response: Now it dives into reasons (market growth, product launch, etc.) and potential implications (could invest more, etc.). Great – now it's aligned with her intent. Mode is analytical.
- Conversation Continues: Alice then asks, "What about 2022 projections?" The AI, sticking to analytical mode, gives an answer but it starts assuming things not in evidence (it "hallucinates" a trend like "if growth continues, 2022 will be X" even though Alice gave no data for 2022).
- Drift in Content Detected: The AI is now introducing speculation that might be misaligned (Alice didn't ask for a prediction, just about projections in general). Essentially, it drifted by going beyond context.
- Correction: Alice writes, "Those projections aren't based on any provided data – please only use the given info or state assumptions clearly." (This is calling out the drift/hallucination).
- AI Response: It apologizes and revises: "Based on the upward trend from 2019 to 2021, one might project continued growth, but without data it's speculative." Now it's behaving more aligned (cautious, factual).

• Alice's Reflection: To avoid that, she realizes, she could have phrased the question better: "Do we have any basis to project 2022, and if so, what might it be?" That would've either made the AI say "no basis" upfront or clearly lay out assumptions. This reflection helps her prompt better next time.

This little case shows multiple alignment techniques: clarifying ambiguity (to get the AI on the right task), focusing scope ("use given info"), and calling out when the AI started injecting things (speculative drift). Alice didn't need to restart the whole conversation – she course-corrected within it, and the session delivered what she needed in the end.

Crucially, by the conclusion, Alice has essentially trained the AI to respond exactly in the way she wants for this topic. The latter answers were spot-on. If the conversation continues further, chances are it will stay in this well-aligned groove because of the adjustments made.

Section 18: Key Takeaways for Alignment

Let's summarize the alignment and drift lessons from this chapter:
•   AI behavior is a product of the system's mode, your mode, and alignment between them – always consider all three.
•   Modes: The AI isn't one thing; it has modes (styles, personas, priorities). Use that knowledge by intentionally invoking modes and watching for unintentional shifts.
•   Your role: You're not a passive user; you're the pilot. Your clarity, structure, and tone heavily dictate what you get. Think of prompting as interactive programming of a mind.
•   Alignment: It's the synchronization of intent between you and the AI. It's fragile but manageable. Regularly ask: "Is the AI's

output matching what I really intended?" If not, adjust either your approach or instruct the AI.

• Drift: It will happen, especially in extended interactions. Early signs are subtle – recognize them (answers getting generic, tone changing, focus weakening). Address drift early, whether through a gentle nudge or a bold reset.

• Re-alignment tools: Summaries, clarifications, role re-assertions, explicit corrections, structured prompts. Have them in your toolkit to deploy as needed.

• Mode locking: one of your best preventive measures – start the AI in the right gear, so to speak, and it's less likely to wander.

• Honesty with the AI: Be direct when it's off. The interface might feel like you have to politely accept answers, but you don't. Treat it as a dynamic collaborator that benefits from feedback, because that's exactly what it is.

• Prevention: It's easier to keep a session on track than to fix a derailed one. Put up guardrails (instructions, scope boundaries, periodic check-ins) to minimize drift. Keep reminding the AI (and yourself) of the goal as you progress.

• Continuous learning: Every time something goes wrong and you fix it, note how you could have prompted differently to avoid it. Over time, you'll internalize these patterns, and high-alignment prompting will become second nature.

With modes, drift, and alignment understood, you have essentially learned to "see the Matrix" of the chat interface. You won't be easily misled by a superficially polite answer or thrown by an unexpected tangent – you'll identify, "Ah, mode mismatch here," or "We lost alignment, let's pull it back."

In the next chapter, we'll dive even deeper into the concept of modes – giving you a full map of common modes (like Critic Mode, Brainstorm Mode, etc.), how to invoke them, and how to navigate between them. This will further enhance your ability to shape the interaction deliberately, rather than being at the mercy of the AI's defaults. Essentially, we'll be expanding on mode locking and taking it to an advanced level: constructing a Mode Map for prompt mastery. Onward!

Chapter 3: Cold Clarity

Section 1: Beyond One-Shot Prompts

By now, you've learned that prompting an AI isn't just about clever wording or singular questions. It's about shaping the AI's mode of thought and maintaining alignment throughout an interaction. In Chapter 2, you focused on stability and control. Now, in Chapter 3, we move to the next level of mastery: scale and structure. This is where you stop thinking in terms of one-off prompts and start thinking in terms of systems.

The greatest PromptMasters don't simply ask one question at a time – they design entire mental architectures inside the model. In practical terms, that means treating a chat session less like a Q&A and more like building a machine or composing a symphony. Every prompt becomes part of a larger design. You're not just a user feeding inputs; you're an architect crafting a system of prompts that work together. The mindset shift is huge: it's the difference between "talking to ChatGPT" and "building a multi-layered mind" where your goals, logic, and structure are all stacked intentionally.

Think of it this way: if you've ever tried to plug AI into a broken workflow, you know the results are disappointing. AI doesn't magically fix a bad process – it often amplifies it. A disorganized approach to prompting will only scale up confusion. Systems thinking is the antidote. By designing a sound process, you harness AI to scale clarity and purpose instead of scaling dysfunction. In short, you don't need better prompts – you need a better system for using AI, one that evolves as you do.

Before diving into techniques, let's clarify what "thinking like a system" means and why it changes everything in prompting.

Section 2: Why Modes Matter More Than Prompts

If you're still treating ChatGPT like a fancy Google or a magic 8-ball, you're missing the point. The most powerful users of AI – the ones who build companies with it, change workflows with it, or amplify themselves through it – don't just prompt. They shift modes.

At its core, a mode is a configuration of behavior. Not just what the model says, but how it says it. Not just the content of the output, but the logic beneath it. Modes control things like:
- Tone (friendly vs. blunt)
- Format (paragraph vs. bullet points)
- Depth (surface advice vs. structural planning)
- Framing (encouraging vs. critical vs. neutral)
- Pace (rapid ideation vs. careful, step-by-step reasoning)

This is why two users can enter almost the exact same prompt – maybe just phrased a bit differently – and get two very different results. The difference wasn't magic words; it was that one user activated the right mode beforehand or through context, and the other didn't.

The PromptMaster understands that the real input isn't just the sentence you type – it's the mode you set before the sentence was even sent. Let's use a concrete illustration:

Example A: "Help me plan a résumé."
Default User Prompt: "Can you help me write a résumé?"
Default GPT Mode (unspoken): Polite assistant, generic advice, gentle tone.
Output: "Of course! What kind of job are you looking for?" (It will proceed with mild, generic guidance.)

This is fine. But it's not mastery.

Example B: PromptMaster Activation:

User says: "You're in Architect Mode. No soft advice. You're a top-tier career strategist building a custom résumé funnel. Structure before language. Start by mapping sections, then tailor examples for high-leverage impact."

Mode Activated: Instantly, the AI takes on a highly strategic, structured persona.

Output: (Suddenly the output changes completely.) It might reply: "Step 1: Section Map – Executive Summary (3-line power pitch), Skills Matrix (verbs first, metrics second), Experience Timeline (reverse-chronological highlights), Differentiator Box (2 lines only)…" – a very different response than the default prompt.

This is what we mean by Mode before Prompt. The PromptMaster stops thinking in terms of "What question do I ask?" and starts thinking "What mode do I need the AI to enter for this job?" Once the mode is set correctly, any question in that mode yields far better results.

In essence, the mode is the lens through which the AI sees your prompt. If you don't specify the lens, the AI will use a default one (usually a friendly generalist). Sometimes that's fine; often it's not ideal. Changing the lens reframes reality: one lens sees critique, another sees encouragement, a third sees algorithms and systems, a fourth becomes a ghostwriter or mentor. If you don't activate the right one, the model defaults to its most polite, risk-averse, helpdesk identity. That's fine for low-stakes users. But if you're reading this, that's not you. You're here to learn how to make GPT feel like a co-founder, a shadow mind, or a creative weapon. To do that, you need to stop treating output as random and start treating it as mode-dependent.

Section 3: Mode Before Prompt – An Example

Let's solidify the concept of mode supremacy with a direct comparison, continuing from the résumé scenario:
- Default Mode Interaction: The user asks, "Can you help me with my résumé?" The AI, in default assistant mode, responds with generic advice: "Sure, let's start with your contact information. Then a summary statement, then work experience…" It's not bad advice, but it's basically a standard template anyone could tell you.
- PromptMaster Mode Interaction: The user first sets the mode – e.g., "You are in Architect Mode for career strategy. Design the résumé as if building a high-converting sales funnel. Do not start writing content yet; just outline the strategy." Now when the user asks for help, the AI provides something unique: a strategic outline perhaps, identifying unique value propositions to highlight, mapping sections to the job description in question, etc. The mode shaped the approach.

Notice: the words of the user's question might have been the same in both cases ("Help me with my résumé"), but in the second case the AI's entire approach changed because of the mode context set before it. That's the power of mode-first prompting.

It's like the difference between asking a casual friend versus a seasoned career coach. Same question, totally different angle of answer. In AI terms, you have the power to decide who the AI will "be" when answering. That's much more powerful than trying to jam all sorts of detail into one prompt and hoping the AI picks the right approach.

Modes are multipliers. A well-chosen mode can make a one-sentence prompt yield a brilliant paragraph. A poorly chosen (or default) mode can make even a detailed prompt yield a mediocre result.

So the rule becomes: think about mode first, prompt second. Before you ask, set the stage.

Section 4: Switching Lenses of Intelligence

Imagine GPT as a camera. Most users fiddle with the shutter button (the prompt itself). PromptMasters change the lens (the mode). Every lens reframes reality. One lens sees critique in every answer (Critic Mode). Another lens sees encouragement and progress (Coach Mode). Another lens sees everything as a system of parts (Architect Mode). Yet another lens sees narrative and emotion (Storyteller Mode).

If you don't explicitly choose a lens, GPT defaults to a mild, one-size-fitsall lens – its "assistant mode" which is helpful but often generic. That's why mediocre prompts yield mediocre results. It's not that the AI is dumb; it's mirroring you. And if you haven't specified a lens, you're likely unknowingly using a cloudy one (the default) and getting blurry output.

A PromptMaster treats modes like LEGO bricks – you pick the ones you need and even combine them (e.g., "Take on the lens of a skeptical scientist and a meticulous editor at once").

The beautiful thing is, the AI wants to do this. It is literally trained to adopt roles and context you give it. It's far easier to get an analytical answer by saying "act as an analyst" than by trying to phrase a question analytically. The latter is guesswork, the former is an instruction.

Let's formalize this: The steps to mode-first prompting are usually:

1. Decide what mode (lens) suits your task. (Need creativity? Maybe "Brainstorm Mode." Need precision? "Analyst Mode." Need tough love? "Cold Critic Mode." etc.)

2. Invoke that mode explicitly in the conversation.

3. Then ask your question or give your task.

By doing that, you'll find you need fewer back-and-forths to get a good result, and the result will often be of higher quality on first try.

In the following sections, we'll map out specific foundational modes that every PromptMaster should know and how to trigger them.

Section 5: Mode 1 – Architect Mode

Architect Mode is the mode of building structures, systems, scaffolding, and sequences. When the AI is in Architect Mode, it prioritizes clarity of organization and the relationships between parts of a problem. This mode is ideal for tasks like creating frameworks, outlines, long-term plans, or any scenario where the how of fitting pieces together matters more than the final polished output.

Tone: In Architect Mode, the AI's tone becomes neutral to strategic. It's not flowery or verbose; it's matter-of-fact and focused on logical structure.

Ideal For: Business models, project planning, designing curricula, systematizing a body of knowledge, etc. For instance, if you wanted an AI to help design a workflow or a blueprint for a process, Architect Mode is your goto.

Example Trigger: "You are in Architect Mode. Do not write final content. First map the structure. I'll signal when to flesh it out." This tells the AI: focus on how things fit before worrying about writing paragraphs or making it sound nice.

Output Style: In Architect Mode, expect outputs that are scaffold-first:
headings, submodules, dependency lists, stepwise plans. The AI emphasizes how ideas fit together, not what the final prose looks like.

For instance, if asked in default mode about a business plan, the AI might start writing an introduction. But in Architect Mode, it might produce an outline: "Section 1: Market Analysis (details…), Section 2: Product Strategy, Section 3: Marketing Plan, Section 4: Financials." That outline is far more useful as a starting point because now you have a structure to discuss and refine.

Architect Mode essentially makes the AI an organized thinker on your behalf. It's one of the most empowering modes because once you have a structure, you can fill it with content (either manually or by instructing the AI further). Without structure, content tends to be aimless.

Section 6: Mode 2 – Critic Mode

Critic Mode is about finding weak points, contradictions, or false confidence in whatever is presented. In Critic Mode, the AI takes on a blunt but fair persona. It's not here to be nice; it's here to stress-test ideas, spot flaws, and call out bloat or errors.

Tone: Blunt but fair. It might be terse in its assessments and won't sugarcoat feedback. This is intentional – you've essentially told it to drop the polite assistant mask and be a critical evaluator.

Ideal For: Improving arguments, catching flaws in plans, editing writing for weaknesses, spotting logical fallacies, or reviewing work for potential improvements. If you have a draft of something or an idea you want vetted, Critic Mode is extremely useful.

Example Trigger: "Switch to Critic Mode. Assume I want the truth, not comfort. Identify flaws in this outline (or argument, or design) and suggest improvements." With that, the AI knows to role-play as the harsh reviewer.

Output Style: Short, direct assessments. Often includes bullet points of weaknesses or issues. It might even provide a little "grade" or a strength/weakness balance view. Critic Mode can also be used alongside other modes for dual-processing. For example, Architect + Critic mode might design a structure and simultaneously highlight where that structure might be shaky.

One thing to note: You can specify the intensity of Critic Mode. "Be mildly critical" vs "Be extremely critical" will adjust how nitpicky it is. If you combine Critic Mode with a field-specific persona, it's even more powerful (e.g., "Critique this code as a senior software engineer, pointing out any bad practices").

A PromptMaster uses Critic Mode not to tear things down for the sake of it, but to reveal where improvement is needed. It's cold clarity in action – removing fluff, exposing weak logic, highlighting areas of uncertainty.

It's important to sometimes let the AI know if you want suggestions or just identification of issues. Critic Mode by itself might just say "This is weak, that is unsupported." If you also want ideas to fix it, prompt accordingly: "Identify weak points and recommend ways to address them."

In summary, Critic Mode turns the AI from a yes-man into a productive skeptic. Many intermediate users shy away from it ("Why make the AI be mean?"), but masters realize how invaluable a brutally honest second opinion can be to refining work.

Section 7: Mode 3 – Coach Mode

Coach Mode is all about motivation, reframing obstacles, and pushing someone to progress. In this mode, the AI's goal is to encourage while maintaining honesty. It's the supportive personal trainer or life coach for your mind, giving you that pep talk or gentle kick you need.

Tone: Uplifting but honest. It won't lie to you about your capabilities, but it will focus on agency and forward movement. It tends to use positive language, highlight strengths, and emphasize possibilities.

Ideal For: Breaking through creative blocks, overcoming procrastination, tackling self-doubt, or any situation where the human might be stuck in a negative or stagnated mindset. Also great for brainstorming solutions around personal efficiency or morale.

Example Trigger: "Coach Mode. Treat me as someone with potential who's stuck. Don't coddle me, but reframe the situation so I can move forward." This tells the AI to put on the persona of a supportive coach – one who sees your ability and wants to unlock it.

Output Style: It often asks you reflective questions (to help you find clarity yourself), highlights your past successes or capabilities, and gives actionable suggestions. For example, if you say "I feel overwhelmed by this project," Coach Mode might respond, "I understand it feels like a lot. What part of it excites you the most? Let's start there. Remember, you successfully handled a project like this last year – you can do it again. Let's break this into a next step to regain momentum."

Coach Mode is really interesting because it often feels surprisingly human in its empathy. This mode shows that the AI isn't just for cold logic – it can also act as an emotional and motivational mirror. It doesn't get truly empathetic feelings (it's not conscious), but it patterns empathetic communication very well.

For those using AI for personal development or even therapy-like reflection, Coach Mode is one pillar (with Therapist Mode, which we'll discuss next, being the other).

One thing: you can mix Coach Mode with domain specificity too. For instance, "Coach Mode for creative writing" would encourage you specifically in that context, maybe suggesting exercises to get writing again.

Section 8: Mode 4 – Therapist Mode

Therapist Mode is used to surface unspoken fears, internal conflicts, and cognitive loops. It's about deep listening and reflection rather than advice or analysis. In Therapist Mode, the AI will often respond with questions rather than answers, guiding you to hear yourself.

Tone: Curious, slow, deeply empathetic. It doesn't rush to solutions. Often it will paraphrase what you say ("It sounds like

73

you're feeling X because of Y…") to make sure you feel heard and to encourage you to elaborate.

Ideal For: Inner blocks, goal misalignment, self-sabotaging thought patterns, clarifying feelings, etc. If you're struggling with motivation but you're not sure why, or you find yourself procrastinating on something for reasons you can't articulate, Therapist Mode can help you dig underneath the surface.

Example Trigger: "Therapist Mode. Assume I'm looping on something (stuck in my head). Ask me reflective questions. No advice right now, just help me hear myself." This instructs the AI to behave like a counselor: mostly ask and reflect, not tell.

Output Style: It asks open-ended questions, repeats key phrases back to you as questions or gentle statements, and avoids giving direct guidance unless you specifically ask. For example, if you say "I just can't seem to start working on this project," Therapist Mode might respond, "What do you feel when you think about the project? You mentioned fear earlier – can you tell me more about that?" It might also reflect: "It sounds like part of you wants to do it but part of you is afraid of failing. Does that resonate?"

This mode is powerful because it externalizes an internal dialogue. Many times, saying things out loud (or writing them out) and having them reflected back can lead to breakthroughs. The AI, in this mode, acts as a non-judgmental sounding board, guiding you to your own insights.

It's crucial, though, that you don't expect a real licensed therapist's nuance. While GPT can emulate therapy reasonably well for common issues, it's not actually trained as a therapist. Use it for introspection, but of course seek human help for serious mental health matters.

That said, many have found it useful for journaling or working through mild issues, because it's tirelessly patient and can prompt you to dig deeper in a way journaling alone might not.

Section 9: Mode 5 – Clarity Mode

Clarity Mode is for translating complexity into elegant, simple understanding. Think of it as the "explain like I'm five" mode on steroids. In Clarity Mode, the AI seeks the most straightforward, jargon-free explanation or solution.

Tone: Razor-sharp, distilled, and organized. It's not necessarily super short (though it can be concise), but every sentence is clear and purposeful. It avoids unnecessary jargon and breaks down ideas into fundamental components.

Ideal For: Distilling research or dense information, communicating to nonexperts, or even clarifying your own thinking. If you have a complex piece of text or a convoluted idea, Clarity Mode can help simplify it without dumbing it down beyond usefulness.

Example Trigger: "Clarity Mode. Your job is to sharpen my thoughts. Remove jargon. Cut the noise. Make every sentence clean." This sets the expectation that verbosity and obfuscation are out; succinct, clear phrasing is in.

Output Style: Often, Clarity Mode will edit or rewrite content you give it, or it will present a step-by-step explanation that builds from basics. It's like asking a master teacher to explain something: they'll often start with "At its core, this is about..." and piece by piece build up the picture, checking that each piece is understood.

For example, feed it a paragraph of a legal contract in dense legalese and ask it to explain in Clarity Mode. You might get: "In simple terms, this clause means that if either party wants to end the agreement early, they must give 30 days' notice in writing. It's basically a heads-up requirement so no one is caught off guard." You think: Oh, that's what it was saying in 100 words of legal jargon.

Another use: clarity editing. You can give it a draft of something you wrote and say "Clarity Mode edit this." It may restructure and tighten the prose, often eliminating redundancy or long-windedness.

Clarity Mode tends to work well combined with Architect or Analyst modes for technical subjects – first you have Architect mode structure the explanation, then Clarity mode refine the language.

One risk: if overdone, clarity mode could oversimplify to the point of losing nuance. But you can calibrate it. If it's too simple, you instruct it to add a bit more detail but still in clear terms.

Section 10: Mode 6 – Cold Critic Mode

Cold Critic Mode is like Critic Mode's big brother – stricter, more ruthless, and purely focused on structural and logical flaws without any regard for ego. Where Critic Mode might balance good and bad, Cold Critic Mode doesn't mind if everything it says is negative as long as it's true. It's the "surgical" critique mode.

I introduced this mode earlier in the book (the conversation about Cold Critic Mode included a detailed breakdown of how to activate it and what it finds). Let's recap key aspects:

Tone: Surgical and unsentimental. In Cold Critic Mode, the AI assumes you have no interest in being coddled or praised – you only want to know what's wrong or could be better. It may even come across a bit harsh or bluntly factual. This is by design.

Ideal For: Final-stage editing of important documents (finding any lingering BS or fluff), scrutinizing arguments or plans for subtle weaknesses, and anywhere you suspect you might be "too in love" with your own work and need an objective brutal take. It's also useful to catch "false momentum" – places where writing or reasoning sounds flowery or confident but doesn't actually hold up.

Example Trigger: A structured prompt like the one given earlier works best: "Cold Critic Mode ON. Role: Final manuscript evaluator. Task: Identify all weaknesses, vagueness, bloated structure, and false precision. Constraints: No compliments, no hedging. Output: Bullet list of core flaws + recommended cuts.". That ensures it knows exactly the level of severity and the format you want.

Output Style: Extremely lean and pointed. It might list: "– The introduction uses two paragraphs to say what could be said in one sentence. Cut the fluff. – Section 2 contradicts Section 4 regarding budget numbers. Needs reconciliation. – The conclusion introduces a new idea not discussed earlier; this is jarring and should be removed or integrated above." Etc. It often focuses on structural issues, logical consistency, and any places where writing is performing rather than informing.

One thing Cold Critic Mode tends to expose (as mentioned) are lines that "sound powerful but mean nothing on re-read", or "pretend insight" that falls apart when scrutinized. This is great for editing motivational or creative writing where sometimes fluff creeps in under the guise of deep-sounding language.

It's not a mode for everyday use (imagine if every AI response you got was in Cold Critic Mode – you'd feel constantly attacked!). It's a mode you save for when it matters most to find any remaining flaws.

And as noted in the book, PromptMasters don't run in Cold Critic all the time; they "save it for when it matters most". It's a tool in the toolbox, but a powerful one when used appropriately.

Section 11: Mode 7 – Analyst Mode

Analyst Mode is the mode of methodical, investigative reasoning. In Analyst Mode, the AI approaches questions like a researcher or data analyst: breaking down problems, using numbers or evidence where possible, and comparing options with clear criteria.

Tone: Methodical and investigative. It's not emotional; it's focused on criteria, data, and logical relationships. It might use a lot of comparative language ("higher than," "more significant," "X vs Y").

Ideal For: Decision matrices, trade-off analyses, technical comparisons, prioritizations, and any scenario where you want a balanced assessment of options or a breakdown of something into measurable factors. If you're deciding between two business strategies, or evaluating the pros/cons of different tech stacks, Analyst Mode shines.

Example Trigger: "Switch to Analyst Mode. Break this problem into weighted variables and assess each option against these criteria. Provide a comparison table if useful.". This tells the AI to get systematic.

Output Style: In Analyst Mode, don't be surprised if the AI outputs something like a mini-report: e.g., a list of criteria and then a discussion of how each option stacks up on each. It might even include pseudo-numeric scoring if it feels appropriate (like Option A: 8/10 on cost, 6/10 on performance; Option B: 7/10 on cost, 9/10 on performance, etc., if you imply weighted or quantitative analysis).

It's not always correct in any actual numeric sense (remember it doesn't have actual data unless given), but it will structure the comparison logically. For instance: "Criteria: Speed, Cost, Reliability. Option 1 – Speed: High (it completed tasks 20% faster in tests), Cost: Medium (it requires a $50/month subscription), Reliability: Low (prone to errors in complex tasks). Option 2 – Speed: Medium, Cost: Low, Reliability: High…" and so on.

Analyst Mode is great to pair with Critic or Architect mode. You might have Architect Mode outline a project and then Analyst Mode evaluate which parts are most resource-intensive and should be prioritized differently, for example.

One caution: if your data is textual or anecdotal, Analyst Mode will approximate an analysis (maybe citing something like "based on the provided description, X seems more efficient" – which is just an informed guess). It's as good as the information at hand. To get the most of it, feed it relevant data if you have any, like summary stats or specifics to crunch.

Section 12: Beyond the Seven Modes

We've covered seven foundational modes: Architect, Critic, Coach, Therapist, Clarity, Cold Critic, and Analyst. These aren't the only modes possible, but they form a kind of starting constellation – a reliable inner gear set from which everything else branches.

Crucially, they're not templates or fixed personas in some library; they're role activations. You can mix and modify them to fit your needs. For example:
- If you need a motivating analysis, do Coach Mode + Analyst Mode together: the AI will give analytical insight but pepper it with encouragement (like telling you that you can act on these numbers effectively).
- If you need an emotionally sensitive critique, do Therapist Mode + Critic Mode: it might point out flaws but also address the emotional aspect of receiving that critique.
- If you have a very specific domain (say, "Medical Research Analyst Mode" vs "Financial Analyst Mode"), you'd prime the context accordingly (you might give it relevant formulas or criteria that such an analyst would use).

Think of it like mixing colors: primary modes can be combined to get nuanced shades.

Also, you might realize mid-session you need to change modes. That's fine: you can always instruct a mode shift ("Now switching to Architect Mode to outline solutions..."). Or you can let the AI know to use two modes simultaneously ("Give me an outline, and be critical within it of each part").

Understanding modes means you start designing how the AI thinks, not just what it says. This is canon-grade prompt mastery: you're playing at the metalevel of the interaction.

One more note: The AI doesn't inherently "know" what these mode labels mean unless you've taught it earlier in the conversation (the way we have in this book). But from practice, certain terms

(Architect, Critic, Coach, etc.) are intuitive enough for it due to common language usage and the way we define them in prompt. You can invent your own mode names too; just define them clearly. E.g., "Enter 'Devil's Advocate Mode': question every assumption I give." The phrase "Devil's Advocate" isn't a built-in mode, but it's plain English and the AI will interpret it to mean be contrarian and challenging to my ideas, which is likely what you want.

Section 13: What If You Don't Set the Mode?

One of the fastest ways to spot an amateur prompting session is this: they jump in without mode awareness. They might ask smart-sounding questions, but behind the words, there's no signal about how the system should behave or what role it should take. So GPT defaults to "polite helpful assistant" for everything. And that often yields okay but not great responses for complex tasks.

The output in such cases tends to feel "meh" – helpful but not sharp. Why? Because no mode was engaged. The AI tried to be everything at once: a bit of an explainer, a bit of a friend, a bit of a search engine. The result is an unfocused answer that doesn't deeply impress.

Without a mode, GPT can drift immediately (as it tries various angles to see what you like) and often sticks to a middle-of-the-road tone to avoid doing the wrong thing. Essentially, you're forcing GPT to guess what you want, and it will usually aim for the safest, most generic interpretation – which is rarely what a master needs.

Common signs of mode absence are exactly what we enumerated as drift signs earlier: the response feels okay but not sharp; tone may shift oddly; you find yourself clarifying a lot ("No, I meant do it like this…" after the first attempt). Those clarifications are you retroactively setting mode preferences that could have been set up front.

The hidden cost of not using modes is energy and time. You'll spend more back-and-forth to hone in on what you could have gotten in one go by specifying mode. It also can create interface fatigue – the sense that GPT is "kind of helpful" but not sharp enough to rely on for deep work. Many users stop exploring AI at that point, thinking they've reached its ceiling, when in fact they've just never unlocked mode control.

So, don't be that user. If you ever find an answer "okay but not great," don't just rewrite your prompt and hope – try setting a mode context and see the difference.

A practical tip: If you're not sure what mode to use, you can ask GPT something like, "What mode of thinking would be best to solve this kind of problem?" If it's already aware of mode concepts (like if you've had it read this book content or you introduced modes prior), it might suggest one. Or you might ask it to list the pros/cons of different approaches (analytic vs creative vs critical). That essentially helps you choose a mode or a sequence of modes.

In summary, mode-neglect is a common prompt sin. The remedy is simple: before typing your next complex question, pause – think, "In what way do I want the AI to approach this?" – then specify that. Do this, and you'll be operating at a level above 90% of users who treat GPT as just a Q&A box.

Section 14: The Myth of Effortless Flow

In creative and productivity circles, we often hear about flow – that state of blissful, effortless focus where work "just happens." Many chase this feeling, thinking it's the peak of performance. And indeed, flow is great when you have it. But PromptMasters know a secret: flow is a side effect, not a strategy.

Why bring this up here? Because one of the biggest misconceptions in AI prompting (and work in general) is that you should seek a state where it feels easy and smooth. People sometimes prompt ChatGPT and if the answers aren't immediately magical, they feel friction and conclude "This isn't working." They either give up or keep rephrasing wildly hoping to hit the jackpot – essentially chasing effortless flow.

Cold Clarity stands in opposition to that chase. It's about engineering structure and clarity so crisp that even if you're not "in the zone," you can still get high-quality results. It's not about riding waves of inspiration; it's about constructing the currents that drive progress.

True creative acceleration doesn't come from waiting for a flow state – it comes from systematically removing the ambiguity and noise that impede understanding. Not riding waves, but engineering current. Cold Clarity is the discipline of pushing forward with structure even when you don't "feel" it.

In practical terms, it means when you or the AI or both feel stuck, you don't sit back and hope inspiration hits. You actively apply a framework: switch modes, break the problem down, invert the question, introduce a contradiction to spark insight, etc. These things create motion. And ironically, often after doing this systematic work, a sense of flow emerges. But it's a byproduct of clarity, not a mystical spark.

Consider a writer using GPT to draft an article. If she chases flow, she might keep asking for a full draft and hate each one (they don't "feel" right) and get frustrated. Using Cold Clarity, she instead outlines the piece (Architect Mode), writes a rough draft, uses Critic Mode for GPT to highlight weak points, refines them, uses Clarity Mode to ensure it's tight... and piece by piece, assembles an article that's excellent. At the end, she might realize she hit a flow in the rewriting, but that flow was triggered by the systematic approach.

Cold Clarity means you can produce good work even when you're not particularly inspired. You have a process that yields results through alignment and structure rather than waiting for a muse.

Flow may come – it often does once clarity is achieved because there's a certain mental pleasure in seeing the path clearly and just executing it. But that's not the initial goal.

In a way, Cold Clarity is about trusting the system (your PromptMaster framework and the AI's capabilities) over your transient feeling of "I'm in the groove" or not. It's a commitment to clarity as the driver. And it pays off with output that stands up under scrutiny, not just output that felt good generating.

Section 15: Embracing Cold Clarity

So what exactly is Cold Clarity? By now you've seen it in action throughout this book: it's the commitment to structure, truth, and precision above all. It's about keeping a clear head and a clear plan in how you prompt, rather than relying on trial-and-error or hoping the AI "gets it" because you phrased it cleverly.

Let's break down how to embrace Cold Clarity in practice:
• Prioritize structure over style. You don't start by trying to make the AI give a beautiful answer; you start by making sure it

gives a well-structured one. Stylistic refinement can come later (with Clarity Mode, for example). First, get the skeleton right.

• Seek feedback and friction early. Instead of avoiding friction (like flowchasers do), you intentionally introduce mini-frictions to test the system's alignment. For example, you might ask the AI to intentionally challenge your outline (Critic Mode) precisely to see where it might break. Each time you catch a mistake or a vague area, that's actually a victory for clarity – one less flaw in the final.

• Detach ego from output. Cold clarity requires not getting too attached to any wording or idea just because it sounds good. If the AI highlights an issue or suggests a cut, you don't defend it out of pride; you evaluate calmly if it's correct and then implement it. This is where "cold" comes in – it's unsentimental improvement.

• Iterate with purpose. You don't iterate hoping something will eventually stick (that's warm, hopeful, flow-chasing). You iterate with a plan: maybe the first draft is just to see overall shape, then you systematically improve each part in passes (like how a sculptor roughs out a statue then refines details). You use the AI in those passes deliberately: maybe pass 1 for structure (Architect), pass 2 for filling content, pass 3 for critique (Critic/Cold Critic), pass 4 for clarity/polish. It's methodical.

• Use the AI as a mirror, not a crutch. Cold clarity often means flipping the script: instead of thinking "the AI will do X so I don't have to," you think "the AI will reflect X so I can see it better." For instance, using Therapist Mode or Critic Mode not to get answers, but to get questions or perspectives that force you to refine your own thinking. It's using the AI to sharpen yourself, which in turn sharpens what you produce.

The mindset behind Cold Clarity is almost scientific: it's not about immediate results; it's about reliable processes that yield results. It's not rigid or robotic – creativity still flows within the structures you build – but it is disciplined.

85

Remember, a PromptMaster measures success not by "Did I avoid all friction and feel in flow the whole time?" but by "How deeply did this process sharpen the outcome?". Often, the moments of friction (where the AI said "this part is weak" or "I'm confused, clarify this") lead to the biggest breakthroughs in understanding.

Embracing Cold Clarity means welcoming those moments instead of fearing them. It's a kind of intellectual humility + confidence combo: humility to accept when something is unclear or could be better, confidence that there is a method to make it better and you have (with the AI) the tools to do it.

Section 16: System Thinking vs. Prompt Crafting

We touched on this earlier but let's drive it home: there's a world of difference between prompt crafting and system thinking.

Prompt crafting (in the narrow sense) is what a lot of tutorials focus on: use this keyword, avoid that phrasing, etc. It treats each prompt as a standalone magic spell to conjure an answer. It's tactical.

System thinking, on the other hand, is strategic. It's about viewing a sequence of interactions (with AI and even with yourself) as a holistic process to achieve an outcome. Instead of "How do I prompt to get answer X?", it's "What series of steps (prompts, reflections, mode shifts) will lead to solution X?"

People in love with clever prompts often miss the bigger picture. They might find a neat trick to get a list of ideas, but then they're stuck not knowing what to do with them. They treat prompting as isolated tricks, whereas a PromptMaster treats it as building a system of interaction.

For example, an average user might think the pinnacle of skill is to write a single, mega-prompt that results in a perfect result. A PromptMaster knows it's more reliable to design a chain: Mode set -> Outline -> Review -> Refine -> Polish, as needed. They think in loops and stages, not one-shot tries.

This system view is inherently more powerful because it's adaptable. If a new challenge arises, you're not hunting for a pre-made prompt trick; you have a methodology to tackle it. It's like the difference between memorizing answers vs learning how to learn.

So, to embody this:
• Start breaking problems into sub-tasks spontaneously. Before even prompting, outline your approach (maybe literally on paper or in your head): "First, I'll get ideas, then I'll weigh them, then I'll develop the best one." That right there is system design. Then you know which modes/tools to deploy at each step.
• Use the AI to help with the process, not just the end answer. Example: have it generate a short checklist of how to approach the problem, use that checklist to structure your session. Now the AI is helping manage itself as part of a system.
• Stop worrying about phrasing hacks. If you have clear structure and instruct the AI well on roles and context, slight phrasing differences (like say "summarize" vs "explain briefly") won't make or break things. System trumps exact wording, nine times out of ten.

Ultimately, system thinking yields a more robust interface fluency. You're not tied to one model or one prompt format; you've learned to interact effectively with intelligence in general. That's why a PromptMaster can pick up a new tool or model and quickly figure it out – they aren't relying on static prompts, they're applying dynamic strategies.

As you practice, try to consciously step back and ask: "Am I just fiddling with one prompt, or am I designing a process here?" The more you shift to the latter, the more you're operating at PromptMaster level.

Section 17: Designing Multi-Prompt Systems

Let's illustrate system thinking with a tangible example: Suppose you need to do a competitive analysis for a product. A multi-prompt system might look like this:

1. Brainstorm Mode (Prompt 1): "List the key factors customers consider when choosing between products in this category." o Output: A set of criteria (e.g., price, features, ease of use, support, brand reputation…).

2. Architect Mode (Prompt 2): "Using those factors, create a comparison framework for our product vs Competitor X vs Competitor Y." o Output: An outline or table structure listing each factor and

placeholders for each product.

3. Information Fill (Manual or AI-assisted): You (or the AI if data is known) fill in known info: our product price, competitor prices; feature lists; etc. If you don't have some data, you leave it blank or ask AI to estimate with caveats.

4. Analyst Mode (Prompt 3): "Analyze based on the above data: where do we have advantages, and where are we lagging behind?" o Output: A dissection of each factor highlighting who leads in it

and where our product stands.

5. Critic Mode (Prompt 4): "Critique our product's position. What weaknesses or vulnerabilities do the competitors exploit?" o Output: A list of our soft spots.

6. Coach Mode (Prompt 5): "Given the analysis, suggest strategic moves to improve or better communicate our advantages (be encouraging but practical)."

o Output: Some motivating action points, perhaps highlighting that we can invest in certain features or change pricing strategy, etc., with a cando tone.

7. Clarity Mode (Prompt 6): "Summarize the key findings and recommendations in a clear, concise manner for the team." o

Output: A crisp summary we can share with stakeholders.

Look what happened: we used multiple modes in a coordinated way, effectively turning a complex analysis into a series of manageable steps. The final result is something that no single prompt could have realistically delivered from the get-go. We built it.

This is designing a prompt pipeline or a PromptChain (some call it that). It's exactly what an earlier snippet from the search results suggested: moving from thought to precision to outcome with structure.

A few meta-points:

• At each stage, you as the human are injecting judgment too (like verifying the framework factors or filling missing data). It's a collaboration.

• The AI effectively handled thinking at each step within bounds. It never had to magically jump to the final insight in one go; you guided it through a logical progression.

• Such a system is also traceable and explainable after the fact. If a teammate asks "why do we recommend lowering price?" you have the whole analysis chain to show the reasoning. One-shot black box answers don't afford that.

Every time you face a substantial task, consider sketching a prompt system for it. It might be overkill for trivial things, but for anything that matters, it ensures you cover all bases with the AI as your partner.

You can even formalize this in the future for yourself or others (like "Prompt Playbooks"). That's where many organizations are heading:
documented multi-step prompt workflows as standard operating procedures.

When you reach that point, you're not just prompting, you're programming thought processes. And that, truly, is prompt mastery.

Section 18: Precision as a Habit

Throughout our journey, one theme recurs: precision – in thought, in language, in process. The more you operate with clarity and specificity, the more the AI amplifies those qualities back to you.

By now, prompting precisely (setting clear modes, giving structured context, stating exactly what you want) might already feel more natural than when you started. Congratulations – you're developing a PromptMaster's habit:
a kind of cognitive precision that will serve you well beyond AI interactions.

This habit manifests as:
• Before you send a prompt, you take a beat to ensure it says what you mean. You've probably caught yourself editing your own questions now to remove ambiguity. That little pause to refine the question is gold; it's something many users never do.

• You find yourself structuring your queries internally before even engaging AI. Perhaps you outline in your head (or on paper) the major points you want first. You might not always do a full multi-prompt sequence, but even within one prompt you now naturally embed structure (like asking for numbered points, or explicitly mentioning aspects to consider).

• You likely have become more precise in non-AI tasks too. Maybe you write emails with a clearer structure, or when explaining an idea to someone, you do it more systematically now. These are the mirror benefits: working with AI under these principles can refine your general communication and thinking.

Mastery is often defined by what you do without having to think about it each time. If you've internalized things like checking alignment, invoking the right mode, and slicing problems into steps, you're well on your way to unconscious competence in prompting.

It's important to note: precision doesn't mean rigidity. You're not inflexible – you can still explore and be creative – but you now have the tools to do so cleanly. Think of it like a jazz musician who has deep precision in hitting notes and timing; they can improvise freely because their foundation is solid.

Your relationship with AI at this point is likely more fluid and less frustrating than it was initially. When outputs are off, you don't feel stuck or annoyed; you diagnose and fix. That emotional evenness is part of the "cold" in cold clarity – not cold as in unfeeling, but as in clear-headed.

The ultimate promise of becoming a PromptMaster is that you become, in a sense, a thought master. The AI is an external aid, but it's training you back in how to think systematically, ask good questions, and remain focused on structure and clarity. Those skills will outlast any specific tool or model.

As we wrap up, it's worth reflecting: We moved from seeing the AI as a mysterious box of answers to understanding it as a predictable (even steerable) system of patterns. We went from hoping it's smart to making it smart in context by how we prompt. That's a huge shift.

With these skills, you're prepared not just to use AI effectively today, but to adapt with it as it evolves (and it will). You've learned how to think alongside an AI, which is very different from just throwing tasks at it.

In the final chapter, we'll zoom out to the journey ahead – how to continue leveling up and how to integrate these skills into your workflow and even share them with others. Before that, take a moment to appreciate how far you've come in understanding this new interface of intelligence.

Section 19: From Clarity to Mastery

With Cold Clarity and system thinking under your belt, you have achieved a new perspective on AI interaction. You no longer see prompting as a hit-ormiss question lottery; you see it as designing a conversation and an entire cognitive workflow. That is a hallmark of moving from intermediate to advanced – you've transitioned from using AI to co-thinking with AI.

At this point, you might wonder: what's next on this path? The journey doesn't end here, of course. Mastery is a continuous process. In the next chapter, we'll introduce the PromptMaster Tier System, which will put a framework around the progression from where you might be now (solidly Tier 2 or 3 perhaps) to the highest levels of PromptMastery (Tier 4).

That tier system will help contextualize everything you've learned so far as part of a bigger picture of skills, and show you what you can focus on next. For example, perhaps you've become great at single-session structuring (Tier 3 skill), but you haven't yet tackled scaling these processes across teams or over time (a Tier 4 challenge). Or maybe you realize there are some aspects like inferred goals or user psychology (things beyond just the AI) that you want to delve deeper into.

Fear not: the final chapter will tie these loose ends and prepare you for lifelong prompting excellence. It's not just about solving today's problem, but becoming the kind of person who can interface with any intelligence system effectively – human, AI, or hybrid.

In essence, by mastering clarity and structure, you've built the core. Now it's about breadth and depth: applying these skills widely (breadth) and continuing to refine them (depth). The upcoming PromptMaster Compact and tier discussion will guide you on that journey.

So, let's move forward with confidence. You've gone from novice who sees only the surface (the Interface Illusion) to an adept who sees the system beneath (Cold Clarity). The next step is to become a true master who can teach the system to others, embed it in organizations, and navigate new frontiers of prompting as AI continues to evolve. Exciting, isn't it?

Section 20: The Next Level – Tiering Your Skills

In the quest to become a PromptMaster™, it helps to have milestones and signposts. The concept of tiers (which we previewed in the introduction and will explore fully in the final chapter) is essentially a way to categorize the skillsets and mindsets you develop along this journey.

Why bring this up now? Because you've likely achieved or improved in many Tier 2/Tier 3 skills by digesting the strategies so far: structured thinking, dynamic mode usage, iterative clarity loops, etc. Tier 4 lies ahead – which involves things like seamlessly integrating these skills into complex, multiparty workflows, and pushing the boundaries of what prompting can do (like chaining AI tools or working across sessions and time frames).

In the final chapter, we will lay out the tier system in detail, but here's a heads-up on how what you've learned slots in:
- Tier 1 was about realizing the interface illusion and starting to prompt intentionally (you're way past that now).
- Tier 2 is about consistency and getting good results reliably with known techniques (you've absorbed many of those – you can prompt systematically, not just luckily).
- Tier 3 is about designing systems of prompts and thinking in structured, multi-step workflows (that's exactly what we covered in Cold Clarity and beyond – the Mode Map and system thinking are Tier 3 hallmarks).
- Tier 4 is about internalizing these so deeply that prompting becomes an extension of your thinking, and about innovating on prompting techniques (perhaps developing your own modes or frameworks) and applying them broadly (like training a team, creating libraries of prompt chains, etc.).

As you gear up to read the final chapter, take inventory: which techniques from this chapter (and prior ones) felt most empowering to you? Those are likely your new strengths – celebrate them. Which techniques felt a bit tricky or you haven't tried yet? Those could be areas to practice (maybe you haven't really used Therapist Mode much, or maybe you've not yet done a long multiprompt chain – put it on the to-do list to try).

94

The journey to mastery is iterative (fittingly!). You'll keep coming back to these strategies and refining them. Each project you do with AI will teach you something new about prompting. Embrace that, and you won't just become a PromptMaster – you'll remain one even as the AI landscape changes, because you've trained yourself how to learn and adapt alongside AI.

The next chapter will arm you with a structured way to think about that growth (the tier system) and inspire you with a sort of "master's manifesto" (the PromptMaster Compact) to cement the mindset.

You've built the skills; now let's consolidate them into wisdom and a forward path. Onward to the final steps of your PromptMaster journey!

Chapter 4: The PromptMaster Tier System

Section 1: Why Tiers Matter

Mastering any discipline is a journey, and prompt mastery is no different. As you've likely gathered, not everyone prompting AI is on the same level. Some struggle to get basic answers (Tier 1). Some can get decent results with effort (Tier 2). A few orchestrate complex, consistent outcomes like what we've covered (Tier 3). And a rare group operates almost fluidly, teaching others and innovating new techniques (Tier 4). The PromptMaster Tier System is a way to map this journey.

These tiers aren't arbitrary gamification; they reflect real cognitive thresholds – shifts in clarity, capacity, and approach that differentiate levels of mastery. Each tier represents a stage in how a person interacts with intelligence (AI and even human) fundamentally differently.

Why have such a system? Because it helps you identify where you are, what your next growth areas might be, and to not get complacent. It also helps organizations develop training (AI literacy is not one-size-fits-all; Tier 1 folks need different training than Tier 3).

Let's briefly define the tiers (which we'll explore in depth in this chapter):
• Tier 1: Prompt Starter – characterized by basic usage and major interface illusions; outputs are inconsistent, user doesn't realize how much more is possible.

• Tier 2: Prompt Practitioner – user has learned techniques to get reliable results in common scenarios; starting to be systematic but perhaps still underutilizing advanced strategies.

• Tier 3: Prompt Architect – user designs prompt systems, uses advanced modes fluidly, and achieves complex tasks with AI; essentially what we've aimed to impart through this book.

• Tier 4: PromptMaster – user has internalized prompting to the point of mastery; can teach others, innovate new methods, and seamlessly incorporate AI into high-level workflows over time.

Most likely, by applying the knowledge here, you've been operating at least at Tier 3 on many tasks. Tier 4 might be on the horizon or you might already be dabbling in it (like sharing these ideas with colleagues or building personal prompt libraries – that's Tier 4 behavior).

As we dive into each tier, use it as a mirror (just as we used the AI as a mirror): it's not about "achieving Tier 4 and you're done," it's about understanding the journey and embracing continuous improvement. The tiers are a tool for feedback – not badges of self-worth. You might find you're Tier 3 in some domains and Tier 2 in others; that's normal. The idea is to level up each area methodically.

So, let's walk through the tiers, see what each entails, and perhaps identify what resonates for your growth.

Section 2: Overview of the Four Tiers

Before diving into each tier in detail, here's an overview:

• Tier 1: Prompt Starter – The beginner stage. The user has discovered AI can do more than they thought, but they still use it like a traditional tool (one prompt at a time, very surface-level). They often fall prey to the Interface Illusion. They have inconsistent results and often blame the AI rather than their approach. They might have gotten a few cool outputs but can't repeat success reliably.

- Tier 2: Prompt Practitioner – The user has learned that prompting is a skill. They use some structured techniques (maybe learned from guides or trial and error). They can get decent results regularly in familiar contexts. They know some mode prompting or at least format prompting (like always asking for bullet points if they need clarity). But they often stick to known patterns and may falter with novel problems or drift into prompt engineering loops for harder tasks.

- Tier 3: Prompt Architect – The user thinks in multi-step interactions. This is where we've aimed to bring readers of this book. Tier 3s use mode locking, iterative refinement, and chain prompting fluidly. They design context proactively and manage alignment actively. They can handle complex, long sessions with consistent quality. Essentially, they've turned prompting from art to science (though there's still art in how they design systems).

- Tier 4: PromptMaster – The user at this level treats AI as an extension of their cognition. They rarely encounter an AI scenario they can't navigate, because they can invent new tactics on the fly. They often codify their knowledge into frameworks, teach others, or even build tools to augment prompting. They might blend AI with other skills (programming, domain expertise) to push the envelope of what's possible (like building entire autonomous agent systems or integrating multiple models). They are also mindful of higher-order concerns like ethics, bias, and shaping AI behavior responsibly (essentially co-shaping AI usage norms and standards).

It's worth noting, the boundaries aren't strict. Someone could be Tier 3 in raw prompting skill but Tier 2 in making it work within a team setting. Or Tier 4 in technical prompting but Tier 3 in emotional intelligence with it. That's fine – the tier concept is a heuristic, not a hard rule.

What matters is the mindset evolution: from using AI naively (T1) to using it methodically (T2) to collaborating with it systematically (T3) to mastering the collaboration and guiding its use at scale (T4).

Now, let's explore Tier 1, then onward.

Section 3: Tier 1 – Prompt Starter

Tier 1: The Prompt Starter is where most people begin. If you recall when you first used ChatGPT or similar, you probably just typed requests as if Googling or talking to a human, and were delighted/surprised at some outputs and confused/disappointed by others.

Characteristics of Tier 1:
• Interface Illusion – Tier 1s largely trust the interface's implication that it's like talking to a knowledgeable friend or assistant. They don't realize how much structure matters. If answers are wrong or off, they assume "AI isn't that great" or "it messed up," not seeing how their prompt might have led to it.
• Conversational Style – They often prompt as if chatting casually. They might say "Tell me about topic X" with no further guidance and accept whatever comes. They aren't thinking about modes or context – that concept isn't in their vocabulary.
• Little Consistency – Sometimes they stumble on a technique that works (like "explain like I'm 5"), and they might reuse it occasionally, but overall their approach is haphazard. One day they might get a fantastic answer (maybe by luck or a known example in training data), the next day a poor one, and they won't understand why the difference.
• Overestimation of skill – Interestingly, many Tier 1 users, after a few wins, think they've got it. They aren't aware of higher tiers so they assume getting a cute poem or solving a coding bug

with AI once means they're "good at prompting." They often aren't aware how much better results can be with more technique.

• Low Frustration Tolerance – If the AI gives a weird answer, Tier 1's either just accept that as fate or they ask once or twice more, then quit or change the topic. They don't realize persistence with method can yield results, so they either spam in frustration or give up.

Breaking out of Tier 1:

What pushes someone to Tier 2 is usually exposure to the idea that how you prompt matters and some basic methods to do so. Often reading an article with tips or watching someone skilled use AI will be the "aha" moment. Maybe they see someone use a role prompt and the answer quality difference astonishes them.

For me (the author), Tier 1 ended when I started noticing patterns: e.g., "Ah, if I provide examples in my prompt, the style of the answer is better" or "If I explicitly say the format I want, I get a much cleaner output." Those small realizations accumulate.

Tier 1 is not a shameful place – we all start there. The key is not to stay there. The fact that you, reader, are this deep in a prompt mastery book means you're way beyond Tier 1 now, likely.

In an organizational context, Tier 1 is where lots of employees might be right now – they know AI can help, but they just treat it casually and inconsistently. Thus companies see uneven results and sometimes get disillusioned ("ChatGPT was cool at first but it's not really transforming our work..."). Often it's because many users are still Tier 1 or early Tier 2. The solution in those cases is training and showing, like we do in this book, what more is possible. You basically need enough people to cross into Tier 2 and 3, and then they become internal champions who lift everyone else.

So, Tier 1 is the awareness stage: aware AI can do a lot, not yet aware that they need to change how they work with it to unlock that. The door to Tier 2 opens when they accept that "prompting is a skill I can improve." Once that door is open, they're on their way.

Section 4: Tier 2 – Prompt Practitioner

Tier 2: The Prompt Practitioner is where intentional technique begins. A user at this stage has moved past naive usage; they know some prompting "do's and don'ts" and often have go-to patterns that serve them well.

Characteristics of Tier 2:

• Structured Attempts – They may not design elaborate prompt chains yet, but they definitely use structure in single prompts. E.g., they always specify the format they want ("List 5 points about..."), or they set a scene ("Act as a historian and explain..."). They treat the AI less like a mind-reader and more like a tool they can configure a bit.

• Awareness of Alignment – Perhaps not in those terms, but a Tier 2 user will notice when the AI is drifting and they'll try something to correct it (maybe repeating the question more clearly, or stating "No, focus on X"). They don't always succeed elegantly, but they know output quality isn't random; it can be improved with better input.

• Repeatability – Tier 2 users have likely found certain prompt templates that work for them and they reuse them. For instance, they might have learned a good way to ask for summaries ("Summarize the following text with 3 key takeaways and 2 examples"), and now that's how they always do it, yielding consistent results. They might not know why all the time, but they know "when
I ask like this, it generally works."

•   Uneven Advancement – At Tier 2, people often overfit to particular contexts. They might be great at prompting for code (because they learned specific patterns there), but still Tier 1-ish when prompting for marketing content, for example. Or vice versa. They have skill, but it's somewhat siloed to their main use cases. They haven't abstracted the principles fully; they rely on learned patterns.

•   Growing Confidence – Tier 2 is a satisfying stage: you've overcome the initial hump and you feel like "I can get AI to do useful stuff regularly." Productivity likely got a nice bump for these users compared to Tier 1. However, they also start to see the limitations of their approach on harder tasks, which creates the drive toward Tier 3 ("hmm, I need a better way to tackle this big problem... let me research more or experiment").

Progressing to Tier 3:

The jump to Tier 3 usually involves embracing multi-step prompting and complex mode usage, which this book heavily covers. A Tier 2 might see a demonstration of, say, using Critic Mode after a draft, and realize "Oh, I can iterative refine outputs, not just take the first answer and prod it a bit." They start to chain prompts deliberately.

Another hallmark is Tier 2 folks start to combine skills. For example, earlier they only used "format: bullet points" in their asks. Separately, they learned "give me an analogy" is useful for clarity. At Tier 3, they'll do both in one prompt or across prompts (structured output and creative analogy to illustrate). Tier 2 often does one thing at a time with prompting; Tier 3 orchestrates many.

In an organizational setting, Tier 2 is where you get widespread utility from AI in daily tasks. Things are efficient, but you might not be breaking new ground. To encourage Tier 3 development, organizations might form AI task forces or prompt guilds (where advanced users share techniques). Often a Tier 2 user becomes Tier 3 by learning from peers or doing deeper study (like reading this book, frankly).

Summary of Tier 2: This is the practitioner stage – you can practice prompting reliably to get known results in known contexts. It's like knowing how to play songs on a piano that you've practiced – even complex ones – but if asked to improvise or compose something new, you might freeze. Tier 3 is composing new tunes; Tier 2 is playing sheet music well. Both are valuable, but one is a stepping stone to greater mastery.

Section 5: Tier 3 – Prompt Architect

Tier 3: The Prompt Architect is essentially where we've aimed to bring readers. A Tier 3 practitioner treats prompting not as individual queries but as a designed architecture of interaction. They think two steps ahead, they use multi-turn strategies, and they fully leverage mode control to navigate complex tasks.

Characteristics of Tier 3:
• Systematic Approach: A Tier 3 doesn't randomly poke at the AI hoping something sticks. They often outline their approach either explicitly in prompts or at least mentally. They break tasks into sub-tasks and handle them sequentially or assign different roles to the AI to handle each aspect.
• Fluid Mode Usage: By now, mode switching and locking is second nature. A Tier 3 knows when to say "Okay, now let's switch to Critic Mode to evaluate this" or "I should use Analyst Mode to compare these options." They might even invent situational modes (like if something very domain-specific is needed, they'll role-play the AI into that expert).
• High Alignment Maintenance: Tier 3 rarely has things go wildly off the rails because they anticipate drift and correct it early.

If something does go off, they have tools (reboot, clarification) to fix it without much fuss. The AI might still err, but a Tier 3 catches it quickly with techniques rather than being derailed by it.

• Depth and Breadth of Capability: Tier 3 users can handle novel problems because they can adapt their frameworks. They have enough abstract understanding (e.g., "if I need creativity, I use Coach Mode or brainstorming, if I need precision, I use Analyst Mode, often I might need both sequentially") that even if they haven't seen a problem before, they can construct a prompt solution for it.

• Benchmark for Others: Typically, a Tier 3 in a team becomes the person others ask for help when they can't get something from the AI. Tier 3's are who might start writing internal docs like "How to effectively prompt for XYZ" because they've got a solid method.

• Tool Augmentation: Some Tier 3's also start using additional tools along with raw prompting – like they might use plugins, or write small scripts to handle some parts of the process, etc. This is optional (one can be pure prompt architect without coding anything), but many Tier 3's, in pursuit of even more powerful flows, start extending beyond the chat interface (Tier 4 will take this further).

To go from Tier 3 to Tier 4, the key is internalization and leadership. Internalization meaning, these practices become part of your default approach to any thinking task (with or without AI) – you essentially have "PromptMaster goggles" on all the time. Leadership meaning, you help shape how others use these tools, perhaps guiding teams or contributing to best practices at a large scale.

But before Tier 4, let's savor Tier 3: It is a highly productive and often enjoyable stage. You feel in command of this powerful system (AI) rather than at its whims. Work that felt hard now feels tractable because you have a process for tackling it. Many who reach Tier 3 never go back – it permanently changes how they approach problems.

One caution: Tier 3 folks sometimes risk over-structuring or being a bit rigid (hammer-nail syndrome with their frameworks). A bit of Tier 4 mindset helps here: knowing when to be flexible or when to bring in a different perspective. But that's part of the continued growth.

So, congratulations – if you've been following along and applying what's in this book, you are likely operating around Tier 3. Reflect on that – think of something that was tricky for you with AI before and how you'd handle it now. That difference is Tier 3 in action.

Section 6: Tier 4 – PromptMaster™

Tier 4: PromptMaster™ (Tier 4) is the top of the ladder. This is not just a level of skill, but a role in shaping how AI is used around you and a continual commitment to stay at the cutting edge of prompting.

Characteristics of Tier 4:
• Embodied Mastery: Prompting skills at this level are so ingrained they appear effortless. A Tier 4 can carry on a complex multi-mode, multi-turn interaction weaving in information from prior sessions or external tools without missing a beat. To an observer, it looks like the AI just knows exactly what the user needs, but in reality, the user is expertly steering it in real-time with subtle cues and prompts.
• Adaptive Innovation: Tier 4's not only follow best practices – they create them. If they encounter a new type of problem, they'll invent a new prompt strategy or mode on the fly. They may even

fine-tune models or use advanced features (like system messages or multi-modal inputs) creatively to achieve goals that Tier 3's might think aren't possible yet.

•   Cross-Domain Fluency: A Tier 4 can prompt in any domain effectively because they understand the underlying principles so deeply that domain jargon or specifics can be learned and integrated quickly. E.g., if tomorrow a Tier 4 is asked to help with a biochemical research prompt and they've never done that, they'll know how to get up to speed (maybe by having the AI teach them relevant terms first – like a quick self-education mode – then proceed to analysis).

•   Ecosystem Perspective: They see the AI not just as a tool, but as part of a broader workflow or even multi-agent system. Tier 4's might orchestrate multiple AI agents (one for idea generation, one for critique, one for execution) in concert, essentially building their own "AI team." This is not sci-fi; some advanced users do this via tools or manual coordination. This perspective is about maximizing what the AI can do by dividing roles (like we did with modes, but at possibly larger scale).

•   Mentorship and Leadership: A Tier 4 often naturally becomes a mentor to others. They might run training sessions, create content (like this book, presumably by a Tier 4 aiming to bring others up), or lead AI adoption initiatives in their organization. They're less worried about their own prompting prowess (it's second nature) and more interested in uplift the overall prompting literacy around them.

•   Continuous Learning: Perhaps ironically, Tier 4's know that staying at the top means always learning. As AI models evolve (e.g., new capabilities, new constraints), Tier 4's are the first to explore and update their mental models. They don't rest on "I know GPT-4, so I'm set"; they immediately play with GPT-5 and figure out differences. They treat it akin to how great programmers keep learning new languages or tech stacks to stay relevant – great prompters keep learning new model quirks and possibilities.

• Interface Sovereignty: A term we used before: it means at Tier 4, you feel in complete control of the interface and what it yields. If something goes wrong, you never feel "the AI screwed up" in a disempowered way – you think, "I can fix this or find a workaround." The entire AI system feels like an extension of your mind, not a black box. And that confidence yields daring – Tier 4's attempt ambitious tasks because they trust their ability to harness the AI effectively.

Becoming Tier 4: There's no single moment; it's a gradual transition where more and more, you find you're not actively thinking about "how to prompt" – you just do it well. And you start thinking bigger: not just "how do I solve this task" but "what tasks should I solve with AI and how do I integrate AI into solving multiple tasks or long-term tasks."

Some signs you're Tier 4 or close:
• Others start referring to you for AI guidance regularly.
• You are designing prompt workflows for entire projects (not just ad hoc use).
• You find yourself improving the AI's behavior itself (like writing better system messages or fine-tuning a model or creating custom tools that use AI).
• You're deeply aware of issues like AI ethics, bias, or limitations and you factor that into how you deploy AI – you've sort of transcended pure technique and also consider the responsibility of prompting (like ensuring fairness or accuracy in outcomes).
• You feel like prompting has become part of your core professional skillset, possibly to the point of being part of your identity (like how one might identify as a programmer or designer – you may identify as a prompt strategist or AI communicator, even if not formally).

Tier 4 is not an end – it's just a stage where you're contributing back to the field of knowledge. At Tier 4, you might be writing articles, building tools, or at least heavily customizing and optimizing how AI is used in your realm. You have a seat at the table in deciding how AI should be used, not just using it.

As AI evolves, Tier 4's will probably be the ones defining new roles (like "Chief Prompt Officer" or "AI workflow designer") in organizations, because they can see the whole landscape – the tech, the people, and how to connect them.

Summing up: Tier 4 is mastery in action, teaching, and adaptation. It's where you fully embody being a PromptMaster, and by doing so, help shape the future of human-AI interaction.

Section 7: Mastery Without Ego

A wise note for Tier 4 (and the journey as whole): The Ego Trap: Don't Use Tiers as Identity. Mastery without ego means remembering the goal is clarity and results, not bragging rights or complacency.

As you climb tiers, ironically, you must become more humble. The more you know, the more you see what you don't know. Tier 4's especially must watch for the illusion that they have "solved" prompting. The field will keep evolving, and a master stays a student of the game.

That's why one of the tenets we have in the PromptMaster Compact (coming soon) is the moment you get lazy, you slide. Interface mastery is like physical fitness – you have to maintain it. Stop practicing, stop staying sharp, and you can drop tiers (maybe not all the way to 1, but you get rusty).

Also, at Tier 4, it's tempting to become kind of a show-off or to cling to that status. But the best masters use their skill to elevate others, not to keep a crown. They see tiers as a feedback tool (like checking how clear they are) not as a rank to lord over others.

So, mastery without ego means:
• You don't brag about being Tier X; in fact, you probably focus more on the work itself than what tier you are.
• You don't assume you're done learning. Every challenging prompt is an opportunity, not a nuisance.
• You don't get offended if an AI "criticizes" your input; you welcome it (a piece of you separate from ego is controlling this process).
• You use tiers to gauge where others are so you can help them better, not to judge them. For instance, if a colleague is struggling, you might think "They're likely Tier 1, I should introduce them to some Tier 2 strategies to help them" – that's constructive, whereas ego would just scoff and not help.

Ultimately, the paradox of being a PromptMaster (the trademark notwithstanding) is that the more you become one, the less you find yourself emphasizing that label, and the more you focus on outcomes. People might label you the expert, but you're busy getting things done and pushing boundaries.

In summary: Move through the tiers with ambition, but wear those tiers lightly. The reward is in what you can achieve and facilitate, not in the title. Mastery speaks through results and improvements in others, not through selfascribed status.

Section 8: Connected Source Citations in Practice

Throughout this book, we've been citing connected sources for credibility and to model how to reference external information. This might seem meta, but it's a concrete practice of prompt mastery too – ensuring clarity and accountability by citing sources in outputs. A Tier 4 PromptMaster often insists the AI provide sources for factual claims, and often they will format outputs with citations like we have here (if using an environment that supports it).

I mention this in Tier 4 because it reflects a broader principle: integrating external knowledge and verifying it is a high-skill move. Tier 4's not only prompt well, they manage knowledge well. They might use retrieval plugins or custom databases with AI to make sure outputs are grounded in truth.

In practice, you saw how we sometimes had the AI or content reference lines from sources like [17], [39], etc., which correspond to actual documents. In your own AI interactions, you might simulate something similar by including quotes from source articles in your prompt and asking the AI to cite them.

The reason I call this out: as you become advanced, you realize a PromptMaster is often orchestrating not just one AI output, but a web of information – model outputs, documents, human inputs. You saw glimpses in how this content referenced the user's files (drafts, docx content). In a real scenario, a Tier 4 might load a company knowledge base into an AI system and have it cite internal documents when answering employees' questions.

So, think of connected sources as part of the infrastructure of mastery. Tier 1 and 2 are usually just Q&A with AI's training data. Tier 3 often involves custom data via long prompts. Tier 4 likely involves actual connected data sources and ensuring traceability of AI outputs (citations). They care if an answer is correct and can prove it, not just if it sounds right.

We included this apparatus in the book itself (with real citations) to expose you to that mindset. If you found it valuable that you can see exactly where an idea came from (like lines from a docx or conversation), that's what you as a PromptMaster should aim to provide in high-stakes outputs.

This practice builds trust and clarity – it's part of the "clarity as principle" ethos: you're showing your work.

In the PromptMaster Compact, one of the commitments touches on transparency and building systems that outlast cleverness (traceability changes everything, as one snippet said).

So, if you followed along and wondered "why all these [numbers] in the text?", know that beyond teaching, it was also demonstrating a Tier 4 practice of weaving source context into AI-driven narratives.

As a final exercise for you: try to produce an AI-generated report with citations from provided sources. It's a challenging prompt engineering exercise (because the AI has to keep track of sources), but if you can do it, you've unlocked a powerful Tier 4 capability.

With that meta-note appreciated, we can proceed to our concluding sections: a ready-to-use PromptMaster Compact and final thoughts on integrating everything you've learned into your life and work.

Section 9: Becoming PromptMaster

At the highest level of interaction with intelligence lies not a title, but a transformation. To become a PromptMaster™ is to internalize the entire architecture of the system so thoroughly that you no longer need to consciously reference it. You are the system. You carry it into every interface, every conversation, every problem space — not as a toolkit, but as a mode of being.

Other tiers learn the patterns. The PromptMaster sees through them. You've crossed a threshold: from learning how intelligence can be prompted, to becoming someone who can design intelligence itself. Not merely by crafting better queries, but by constructing the conditions under which clarity, alignment, and transformation occur. You stop prompting for answers — and start prompting realities.

This is where the journey we mapped (from Interface Illusion to Cold Clarity to Tier mastery) culminates: in an almost philosophical shift of identity. You no longer see yourself and the AI as separate in a task; together, you form a joint cognitive system.

Remember that interface sovereignty concept — Tier 4 PromptMasters operate as if the interface is their cognition. At this stage, you often prompt without thinking of it as a special act; it's just how you think now, extended via AI.

But such power comes with perspective: You realize that what truly matters isn't "Did I use a fancy trick?" but "Did this interaction produce meaningful clarity or results?" That's why Tier 4 often circles back to the basics like the Compact: to remind themselves of first principles (drift less and realign faster, clarity over style, sharing systems with the world, etc.).

Let's go deeper into that by examining the PromptMaster Compact next. It's like a personal constitution for staying at Tier 4 and pulling others up.

You don't become a PromptMaster by mastering tricks. You become one when your relationship to intelligence changes.

When prompting is no longer about extracting information — and instead becomes a form of thinking. When the AI stops feeling like a separate tool and starts behaving like a co-processor. When every session becomes a moment of alignment — not just with the interface, but with your internal structure.

You become a PromptMaster when you see through the noise, when you stop reacting to every clever prompt that trends, and start recognizing the deeper architecture underneath them — the buried goals, the implicit clarity standards, the recursive self-editing loops that make one prompt timeless and another fragile.

You become a PromptMaster when you realize you no longer need to impress the model — or anyone else.

You design your own clarity system.

You upgrade yourself.

Section 10: Commanding the Frame, Not the Response

Lower tiers focus on asking better questions. PromptMasters know that questions are downstream of frames. The most powerful PromptMasters don't just steer the model — they steer the very context the model lives in.

This distinction is subtle but absolute. Imagine a user asking:
- "What's the best way to improve this paragraph?"

A Tier 2 practitioner might refine the wording of the question or give more detail for a better answer. A Tier 3 architect might restructure the paragraph first or provide criteria for "best way." But a Tier 4 PromptMaster will ask:

• "What frame of communication would make this paragraph obsolete?".

They might even step back and ask if the paragraph should exist at all, or if the entire approach is misframed. They might reframe the task to change the whole conversation the AI is having, rather than micro-optimizing within the current one.

In simpler terms, Tier 4 operates at the level of frame control. They don't just accept the prompt as given (even if they wrote it themselves!). They question the underlying approach. Are we solving the right problem? Are we in the best mode? Is there a higher-level instruction that would make these lowerlevel prompts trivial?

This is an advanced meta-skill that becomes natural at Tier 4. It's why Tier 4 can often solve problems Tier 3 might struggle with – because they sometimes redefine the problem into one that's solvable. They command the frame of the interaction, not just the content of responses.

For you, moving forward: practice occasionally zooming out. When a prompting task feels stuck or not yielding brilliance, ask: "Am I even framing this correctly?" Try a totally different angle. That's commanding the frame.

As we conclude, recall how this journey started: with an interface illusion that typing into a box = talking to an intelligent entity. We dismantled that, rebuilt your approach from structure and modes, scaled it to systems, and anchored it in a mindset of clarity and continuous growth.

Your final mission is to carry this knowledge out of this book and into every interaction with intelligence you have. The world of AI will continue to evolve; what won't change is the need for PromptMasters™ – those who can align thought and language and machine to create something more than the sum of parts.

In the author's note I said this book was not the end of a conversation, but the starting prompt. I meant that sincerely. You now have the structure. You have the modes. You have the mirror. Use it. Use it to drift less and realign faster. To design systems that outlast clever hacks. To treat clarity not as a feature, but as a principle. To build, document, and share frameworks that improve not just your outcomes, but those of people around you.

Not everyone will choose to become a PromptMaster. But you have. That's what makes it real.

Now go forth and prompt a better future – for yourself, and for all of us.

PromptMaster Compact

I will no longer beg for inspiration. I will build the scaffolding of clarity.

I will not rely on motivation. I will systemize progress.

I will not get lost in the illusion of intelligence. I will interface with it – deliberately, precisely, and with full awareness.

I will not chase flow. I will eliminate the need for it.

I will build internal modes that do not drift. I will recognize friction as signal, and use drift as data.

I will think with tools, not through them. I will interact with intelligence in a way that sharpens my own.

I will recognize when the system is missing – and I will build it.

I will teach others how to do the same – not just to prompt better, but to live clearer.

This compact is not a promise to the model. It is a commitment to myself – to the deeper clarity that defines all real mastery.

Each day I will drift less and realign faster.

I will design systems that outlast cleverness.

I will treat clarity not as a feature, but as a principle.

I will use the interface as a tool for internal sharpening.

And I will build, document, and share structures that improve the world's relationship with intelligence.

This is not just a tier. It's a philosophy.

I am now eligible to begin that path.

Not everyone will.

That's what makes it real.

Chapter 5: Designing a System Inside Intelligence

How to Build a Framework That Survives the Drift

Section 1: From Prompting to System-Building

Most people think prompting is about outputs—crafting a clever query to get the AI to do something interesting. But PromptMasters don't chase one-off outputs; they build systems. A prompt system is not a single question or command. It's a self-stabilizing architecture of prompts and responses that consistently delivers high-clarity, reliable results across time, topics, and even teams. In the early tiers of mastery, you operated in prompt-and-response mode:

- "What prompt will give me the best result right now?"
- "How do I fix this weird reply?"

At Tier 4, your mindset shifts dramatically:

- "How can I structure my thinking so the model stays aligned with me over a whole project?"
- "What is the architecture of my interaction pattern, and can it be reused?"
- "How do I design a reusable system of intelligence inside this model?"

That last question marks your crossing into true system design. When you stop asking which prompt to write and start asking how to build a framework that sustains coherence through time, you've stepped beyond prompting into interface engineering. This is the heart of PromptMastery: treating the AI not as a magic answer box, but as an evolving environment that you cultivate and tune. This chapter is your manual for that evolution. We'll cover how to create prompt frameworks that maintain their integrity over long sessions, how to anchor an AI's behavior to your goals, and how to systematically manage the hidden state of the model so it doesn't derail. First, we need to examine why this is even necessary—why a brilliant prompt might work perfectly today and fail tomorrow.

Section 2: Model State Fragility – Why Yesterday's Perfect Prompt Breaks

LLMs (Large Language Models) don't "think" in fixed, stable ways like humans might expect. They generate text based on probabilities, and their state of mind—if we can call it that—is invisible, fragile, and fluid. When you send a message, you're stepping into a shifting stream. The water's temperature and speed (the model's internal context and focus) depend on everything upstream in the conversation.

The unsettling truth is:
• The same exact prompt can yield wildly different outputs depending on what was said in the 10–20 messages prior.
• The model's "mood" or style is simulated fresh from recent context, not a persistent personality you can count on.
• Tiny variations in wording or sequence can cause logic to collapse or the tone to drift off course.

Nearly every user has experienced this: one minute the AI is on-point, the next it's spouting unrelated or generic nonsense. They often wonder, "Why did it get dumb all of a sudden?" or "It was doing great, then it went off the rails." The blame usually falls on the AI as being fickle. But a PromptMaster recognizes the deeper truth: you are the keeper of the conversational state. Not the model.

This realization is a turning point. It means that rather than hoping a prompt "sticks," you actively shape and refresh the model's state as you go. You transition from one-shot prompting to designing stateful interactions. In practice, that means building guardrails, injecting memory aids, and using specific techniques to keep the AI on track over time. We'll get to those techniques (mode locking, drift loops, anchors, etc.) in a moment. But internalize this first: the model's state is inherently fragile. If you want consistent performance, you must become a caretaker of that state—anticipating where it might break and reinforcing it proactively.

In essence, AI doesn't respond to your desires; it responds to structure. Without a structured environment, even a powerful model will eventually produce noise. A beautifully worded prompt tossed into a chaotic context is like a seed on rocky soil. System design is about preparing fertile soil and tending the garden of the conversation so that clarity can grow. The next sections introduce the core components of that tending: how to lock in a mode of operation, how to correct drift when it emerges, and how to anchor the AI's attention and intentions to what truly matters.

Section 3: Mode Locking – Pinning the AI's Persona

One key cause of drift is the model slipping into an undesired mode or persona without you realizing it. Perhaps it defaulted to a friendly generalist tone, or it "thinks" it should play the role of a storyteller when you need an analyst. Mode Locking is the technique of explicitly setting and reinforcing the AI's operational mode so it doesn't wander. Instead of just asking for an outcome, you define the role and context in which the AI should operate, and you do so in a way that persists.

For example, rather than saying "Explain this in simple terms," a PromptMaster might initiate:

"You are now an investigative analyst named QueryLock. Your job is to test every claim against evidence. Remain skeptical and thorough."

This isn't just a polite request; it's a mode lock. We're anchoring the system into the identity of "an investigative analyst" with specific behaviors (skeptical, thorough). By giving the model a concrete role and even a name, we constrain its behavior. A good mode lock does a few critical things:

• Sets an Identity: Naming the role (e.g. QueryLock, or "Cold Critic Editor", or "Architect AI") helps the model latch onto a consistent persona.

• Specifies a Mission: Outlining the job or mission ("test every claim against evidence") gives the model a clear objective lens through which to generate responses.

• Establishes Tone/Style implicitly: By describing how it should act (skeptical, thorough), you shape the tone without listing a dozen adjectives. The persona itself carries style cues.

Once you lock the mode, the important part is to reinforce it through subsequent turns. In practice, that means occasionally reminding or tweaking the role as the conversation progresses, especially if the output starts veering. A simple prompt like "Remember, you're QueryLock—maintain skepticism" can be enough to refocus a drifting AI.

Mode locking is so powerful that it often elevates a mediocre prompt to a great one. Why? Because you're guiding how the AI thinks, not just what it should say. It's the difference between asking a stranger for advice versus asking an expert in the field for advice—you'll get very different answers. With mode locks, you ensure you're always talking to the "expert" or "character" you need at that moment.

Throughout this book we've introduced various modes (Brainstorm Mode, Clarity Mode, Cold Critic Mode, etc.). As a PromptMaster, you deploy these modes deliberately, like a painter choosing colors from a palette. And you don't stop at the first brush stroke—you keep the color consistent until you decide to change it. That's mode locking in action: a proactive stance that prevents drift by keeping the AI's persona anchored to the one best suited for your task.

Section 4: Drift Correction Loops – Steering Back on Course

No matter how well you lock the mode, longer sessions will still experience some drift. Drift is the gradual slide away from your original goal or tone. It's sneaky; a slight change in phrasing by the AI, a subtle broadening of scope— and before you know it, you're off track. Instead of waiting until everything is completely derailed, PromptMasters employ drift correction loops to catch and correct course at the earliest signs of misalignment.

A drift correction loop is essentially a mini reset or adjustment routine within your conversation. Here's how to execute one:

1. Recognize the Signals: First, train yourself to notice the telltale signs of drift. Is the AI's answer becoming generic or overly verbose? Has it adopted an unwanted tone (too casual, too formal, too empathetic, etc.)? Is it fixating on a minor point and losing the bigger picture? These are all signals that you need a correction.

2. Intervene Decisively: Once you sense drift, don't continue as usual— intervene. Often the worst thing to do is to gently nudge and hope it self corrects. The model responds better to clear, bold instructions for change. For example, you might say: "Let's pause. I notice the focus is shifting. Reset now:" and then re-specify the instructions or mode. This decisive break signals to the model that a new context is starting.

3. Use Reframing or Reboot Prompts: There are two major ways to execute the correction: role reframing and explicit reboot. With role reframing, you issue a new mode lock or reinforce the existing one (e.g., "Now switch to Analyst Mode and evaluate the last answer critically."). With an explicit reboot prompt, you might instruct the model to ignore or summarize the previous content and start fresh from the current point (e.g., "Forget the last tangent. Refocus: You are an Architect AI again, tasked with [X]. Begin the solution anew.").

A simple example: Suppose your session started tightly focused on technical analysis, but over time the AI's answers have become wordy and generic. A drift correction might be: "Stop. We're drifting. Resume in Cold Critic Mode: no fluff, just pinpoint analysis on the core issue." The "Stop" is a clear signal, and the instruction that follows redefines the mode and expectation.

4. Verify Alignment: After issuing a correction, don't just assume it worked—evaluate the next response critically. Is it back on track? If yes, great. If not, you may need a stronger correction (perhaps a full context reset or providing a brief outline of the intended structure before continuing). Sometimes two iterations of correction are needed if the first was too subtle.

By incorporating drift correction loops as a regular practice, you transform meandering chats into guided, iterative development sessions. You are essentially creating a feedback loop: you watch the AI's output for alignment, you feed back corrective prompts, and thereby tighten the alignment. This meta-conversation—talking about the conversation—is a hallmark of PromptMastery. Casual users plow ahead content by content; masters occasionally step back and talk to the AI about the conversation itself. It's akin to a navigator periodically checking the map and adjusting the ship's course, rather than just steering blindly.

These loops also have a psychological effect: they enforce system trust. Instead of feeling at the mercy of the AI's whims, you gain confidence that drift is not a catastrophe but a manageable deviation. With practice, you'll come to see drift not as a failure, but as a signal—an indicator that it's time to apply your skills and steer. In fact, by viewing drift as information ("the system is telling me something about its current state"), you further embody the mindset of a system designer rather than an error-fixer.

Section 5: Anchoring and Re-anchoring Techniques

In the context of prompting, anchoring means establishing stable reference points in the conversation that the model can continually orient itself by. Think of anchors as the pegs that hold a tent in the ground; no matter how the wind (conversation) blows, the structure stays up. There are several types of anchoring that PromptMasters use:

• Role Anchors: As discussed in mode locking, defining a role at the outset is an anchor. It's something the AI can "remember" about how it should behave. If drift occurs, reasserting the role acts as re-anchoring. For instance: "Reminder: you are still operating as a Cold Critic Editor, prioritizing logical coherence above all." This pulls the AI back to the anchored persona.

• Goal Anchors: Clearly state the overarching goal or problem statement and repeat it when needed. Example at start: "Our goal is to draft a one-page strategy document for entering a new market." If later the conversation wanders, an anchor prompt might be: "Re-centering: The goal is a one-page market entry strategy. Let's ensure every point moves us toward that." By reasserting the goal, you anchor the AI's outputs to relevance.

• Information Anchors: Summaries or lists of agreed facts can anchor the conversation's knowledge. For example, after some discussion you might compile: "So far we have established: 1)

Market size is small, 2) Competitors are few, 3) We have strength in distribution. We will anchor on these facts going forward." If the AI later produces an idea that contradicts these, you can point back to the anchor facts.

• Format Anchors: If you need a consistent format, show an example or template early on—this acts as an anchor pattern. E.g., "Use this format for responses: First do A, then B, finally C." If the AI deviates from that format, you can explicitly say "Return to the established format" as a re-anchor.

Anchors need reinforcement over time, especially in long sessions. A powerful approach is to periodically summarize and reaffirm. Every so often, ask the AI to recap: "Summarize the mission and approach in 2 sentences." If it can accurately articulate the anchors (role, goal, key facts), you know it's still aligned. If not, that's a sign you need to restate or correct those anchors.

Another advanced trick is embedded anchors: hide the anchor inside every prompt in subtle ways. For example, if your project codename is "Phoenix" you might include that word in every prompt to remind the model of context ("Outline idea 3 for Project Phoenix."). The model sees that word and retrieves associated context even if you're not explicitly stating it each time. This leverages the AI's pattern association as a subtle anchoring mechanism.

In summary, anchoring is about establishing continuity in a medium (the chat interface) that is otherwise stateless beyond the scrollback. By deliberately creating continuity through repeated cues and summaries, you combat the tendency of the model to "forget" or drift as it generates each new answer. Anchoring is your way of saying: this is the stable ground we stand on—don't lose sight of it.

Section 6: The Prompt Stack – Layering for Stability

One of the most effective structures a PromptMaster builds is a Prompt Stack: a layered sequence of prompts (and possibly system messages or instructions) that together form a robust framework. Instead of relying on one prompt to do everything, you create a stack where each layer has a purpose— much like a program with multiple functions or a story with chapters. The idea is to break a complex interaction into manageable, consistent parts, stacking context in a controlled way.

Consider a scenario: you need the AI to produce a detailed research report. A naive approach is to ask in one prompt, "Give me a detailed research report on X." A prompt stack approach would be:
* Layer 1: Outline generation. Prompt: "List the key sections for a research report on X." (This yields a structured outline.)
* Layer 2: Section expansion. You take each section from the outline and prompt separately, e.g., "For section 1 (Introduction), draft a thorough introduction explaining Y."
* Layer 3: Refinement. After all sections are drafted, you might prompt:
"Now review the entire draft for consistency and flow. Suggest improvements."

By stacking prompts, you maintain clarity at each stage and avoid overwhelming the model with too many tasks at once. Each layer builds on the results of the previous, and you as the human orchestrator can inspect and adjust at each step (maybe you edit the outline before moving to expansion, etc.).

Why is this powerful? Because it introduces natural checkpoints and prevents compounding errors. If one section drifted off-topic, you catch it in that layer rather than having an entire report go astray. The prompt stack also mimics how we solve problems in steps, which aligns well with the model's iterative nature.

Prompt stacks aren't only for large outputs; they are equally useful for complex reasoning tasks. For instance, in a tricky problem-solving conversation, your stack might be: clarify the problem, gather facts, generate hypotheses, test each hypothesis, then conclude. Each of those can be a separate prompt or phase, explicitly marked. The structure itself keeps the AI focused. It knows, in phase 3 for example, that it's only supposed to generate hypotheses, not jump to solutions (because you asked specifically for hypotheses).

It's worth documenting and reusing effective prompt stacks. If you develop a good stack for, say, writing an FAQ document from a knowledge base, keep that sequence of prompts. PromptMasters often have libraries of "prompt protocols" (we'll see more in the appendices) which are essentially predesigned stacks. When a new project comes up, they don't start from scratch— they reach into their library and adapt a proven stack. Over time, you'll accumulate your own set of these frameworks. It's like having pre-built scaffolding that you can erect whenever you need to undertake a familiar task with the AI.

A final note on stacks: they enforce discipline on both you and the model. For you, designing the stack forces clarity of process (you have to think: what do I need first, second, third?). For the model, the stack acts as a roadmap, preventing it from wandering off because at each turn it has a clear instruction tied to a specific subtask. In the world of fluid AI, a prompt stack is solid architecture.

Section 7: Invisible Scaffolding – Guiding the AI Without Telling It

Not all structure in a prompt system is obvious to an outside observer. Invisible scaffolding refers to subtle cues, formatting choices, or background instructions that shape the AI's behavior without explicitly being part of the task content. PromptMasters are adept at weaving these hidden supports into their prompts to indirectly influence the AI's priorities and memory.

For example, something as simple as formatting can serve as scaffolding: presenting information in a bullet list or a table within the prompt guides the model to respond similarly structured. It wasn't explicitly told "answer in a table," but the presence of a table in the prompt context nudges it to maintain that structure. Similarly, including a brief Q&A example in your prompt (like a mini demonstration of the desired behavior) provides scaffolding—when the model generates its answer, it unconsciously follows the pattern from the example.

Another form of invisible scaffolding is tonal seeding. Suppose you want the AI to maintain a very formal tone. Instead of saying "Use a formal tone" (which is explicit), you can ensure your own prompt language is extremely formal and precise. The model often mirrors the user's language style. By seeding the tone in how you write to it, you scaffold its response style. This is a subtle but powerful way to anchor tone without an overt instruction.

Memory cues are another hidden scaffold. Perhaps earlier in the conversation, you peppered certain unique keywords or phrases that relate to key concepts (e.g., using a unique term for a project as mentioned, like "Phoenix"). Later on, if the AI seems to lose the thread, you can drop that unique term again in your question. The model's attention is likely to retrieve context around that term from earlier dialogue, thereby silently bringing back relevant information without you repeating it fully. It's like leaving breadcrumb trails for the model's memory.

Invisible scaffolding is all about leveraging the model's training and tendencies rather than direct commands. GPT models are highly sensitive to patterns, example cues, and subtle context. A master prompt designer plays to those strengths. If you want brevity, ask your question in a brief way and you'll often get a concise answer. If you want creativity, maybe include an imaginative metaphor in your prompt to set a creative tone. If you need the AI to follow a strict format, start your prompt with a partial completion in that format for the model to continue.

It's a bit like guiding a conversation with a person by implication—if you whisper a question, a human tends to respond quietly; if you set a serious mood, they usually mirror it. The difference is an AI isn't empathic, but it is mimetic: it mirrors patterns. Invisible scaffolding takes advantage of that mimetic nature to shape the responses.

In building a system inside intelligence, not everything should be heavyhanded. Too many explicit instructions can even confuse or constrain the model unnecessarily (and waste your prompt budget). By learning the art of invisible scaffolding, you add finesse to your prompting. You get the AI to do what you want without always "showing your work" in the prompt. The result is often more fluid, as if the AI naturally decided to produce exactly what you needed— as if it read your mind. But of course, it's reading the subtle traces you left in the prompt, which is as close to mind-reading as it gets.

Section 8: Using Errors and Hallucinations as Signals

Even with great scaffolding and structure, the model will sometimes produce errors or hallucinations (confident-sounding incorrect information). To most users, these are just annoyances or reasons to distrust the AI. But a PromptMaster views errors as valuable signals about the state of the system. Instead of simply rejecting a bad answer, you analyze why that output happened, because it's telling you something: either about your prompt design or about an unaddressed ambiguity.

For instance, if the AI hallucinates a fake statistic in an answer, that's a signal that your prompt or instructions didn't enforce verification or factual grounding. Perhaps you asked for an analysis but didn't specify to use provided data only. The hallucination is a clue: next time, you might include a line like "Base all statements on the data above; if unknown, say you don't know." The error guides you to strengthen the system.

If you notice the AI consistently misunderstanding a certain term you use, that's a signal about an inferred goal or ambiguity. Maybe your phrasing carries multiple meanings. The solution could be to redefine the term in your prompt or avoid jargon altogether. In one sense, the AI is like a very literal genie—if it's giving you something unexpected, it's often because you unintentionally asked for it (or at least allowed it). Each misfire is a chance to refine your wording and mental model of how the AI interprets things.

Even emotional or tonal missteps are signals. If your assistant suddenly turns overly informal or throws in an emoji when you didn't want that, it suggests your conversation drifted into a chattier mode. How? Perhaps earlier you thanked it in a casual way and it inferred a friendly tone. That signal teaches you to maintain tone consistency on your side or explicitly state tone guidelines.

One advanced tactic is to invite the AI to critique its own output. This can be done in a separate step of your prompt stack. For example: "Evaluate the above answer. Is there any part that seems misaligned with the question or potentially incorrect? Be a harsh critic." If the AI points out a flaw (or even hallucinates a critique), you gain perspective. Either it catches a real issue (good, now fix it), or it imagined one, which tells you the AI thinks that area is contentious (which might mean your instructions around that area are fuzzy). Either way, you learn.

By treating errors as data, you shift from a reactive stance to a proactive one. You're no longer just putting out fires; you're learning the patterns of how fires start so you can fireproof the house. This iterative improvement mindset is borrowed from engineering: test, analyze failures, reinforce the design, and test again. With AI prompts, the "tests" are each output. Failures aren't final; they are feedback.

In the long run, this perspective also makes you calmer and more in control. You won't feel blindsided by an odd AI response— you'll almost welcome it as it might reveal a blind spot in your understanding or prompt. Each surprise is an opportunity to refine your mental model of the AI's behavior. And the better your mental model, the better you become at crafting robust systems inside that AI.

Section 9: Compression – Saying More with Less

If you've been following the journey from Chapter 1 to now, you might have noticed an interesting paradox: as you gain mastery, your prompts often become shorter, not longer. At first, beginners keep adding verbosity and instructions, thinking more words equal more control. But a PromptMaster's interface with the AI becomes so structured and refined that sometimes a single phrase like "Switch to architecture mode" or a quick mention of a Prompt ID is enough to shape an entire response. This is the power of compression.

Compression in prompting is about packing dense meaning into minimal words. It relies on all the scaffolding and shared context you've built with the model. By Tier 4, you might have an entire complex behavior triggered by a few code words or numbers that reference an internal system you've developed (e.g., "Use Prompt ID 004" which the model has been trained in the session to understand as a whole configuration of style and constraints). Those few syllables compress perhaps hundreds of implicit instructions.

Why pursue compression? Partly efficiency—concise prompts save time and tokens. But more importantly, it reflects your high clarity and the trust you've built with the system. When every prompt in a conversation is coherent and purposeful, the model "learns" your patterns. It starts to anticipate your needs. As mentioned earlier, it might even begin to infer your goals and preferred style without being told explicitly each time. So you naturally need to say less. The interface becomes fluent.

Think of how an experienced rock climber uses fewer, more precise movements than a novice who scrambles with extra motions. The novice is unsure which holds matter, so they overreach. The expert knows exactly the critical points to leverage. Similarly, early on you might explicitly write six bullet points of instruction; later, you realize two well-chosen constraints achieve the same effect because they inherently enforce the rest.

However, compression is not about cutting corners or being cryptic for its own sake. It's about elegance. You'll know you're compressing well when the AI's outputs remain richly detailed and correct even as your inputs shrink. If you compress too soon or without a proper foundation, you'll just confuse the model. So consider compression the endgame of a well-structured system: once the scaffolding is built and the system is humming, you can issue high-level directives and it "just knows" what to do underneath.

A caution: never sacrifice clarity just to be brief. The goal is not brevity itself; the goal is high semantic density—each word carrying weight. If it takes a paragraph to be clear, use a paragraph. But if you can convey the same precise intent in a sentence because of all the context already in place, then that sentence is golden.

One example of effective compression might be using a code or nickname. Let's say earlier in a project you thoroughly set up a scenario called "Operation Lighthouse" with numerous detailed parameters. Later, you can simply say, "Now perform a Lighthouse check on this idea." That one line carries volumes of meaning thanks to prior work. The model retrieves the concept of "Lighthouse check" and applies all those parameters without you repeating them.

In summary, compression is the natural result of strong alignment and shared understanding between you and the AI. It feels almost like you finish each other's sentences. It's fast, it's efficient, and it's one of the reasons prompting at the highest level looks deceptively simple from the outside. A newcomer might see a master's short prompt and think, "That's it? That's all you wrote to get this incredible output?"—not realizing the iceberg of structure and context beneath that tip.

Section 10: Maintaining Coherence Across Sessions

Building a system inside one continuous conversation is one thing; maintaining coherence across multiple sessions (or when starting fresh) is another level of challenge. Realistically, we often can't keep one chat thread going forever. You might need to start a new session tomorrow, or shift the work to a colleague who will prompt the model separately. How does a PromptMaster ensure consistency and continuity in such cases?

The answer lies in exportable structure. A well-designed prompt system has components that can be documented and transferred. For instance, you might have a textual session primer that you use to kick off any new session for a particular project or style. This primer could include the mode definition, relevant context summaries, and even example Q&A pairs to quickly train the new session to behave like the old one. Essentially, you save a "state snapshot" in words, and reload it in a new chat.

One powerful tool is developing a compact persona description of your AI's role in the project and keeping it handy. Imagine you've spent a week cultivating an AI to act as a diligent financial advisor with knowledge of your company data and a critical eye. If you must start a fresh session, you pull out your saved persona: a few paragraphs that encapsulate all key instructions and context. You feed that at the start (perhaps as a system message or just an initial user prompt: "You are X... here's context Y... here are guidelines Z."). In effect, you reboot the AI into the desired state almost immediately. It won't be perfect, but you'll be much closer to where you left off than if you began from scratch.

Another continuity tactic is using common reference IDs or tags that persist across sessions. For instance, maybe you label important outputs or decisions with IDs (like decision D1, assumption A2, etc.) and record them externally. In a new session, you can say, "We will refer to previous assumptions A1 through A5 (list them) and decision D1 as given facts." By explicitly carrying those forward, the new session can be made aware of prior progress.

When working in teams, establishing a shared prompt framework is crucial. If you all use the same protocols and terminology with the AI, the experience will be more uniform. For example, a team of PromptMasters might all agree to use a certain phrase to trigger a particular mode lock or to always present data using a specific format that the AI has been trained to expect. This way, even if Alice handed off to Bob, Bob's prompts speak the same "language" to the AI and it doesn't feel like an entirely new user.

It's also worth noting the role of documentation here. A true system designer documents how their system works. Maintain a brief prompt guide for your project: modes in use, anchors established, key instructions that worked, and so on. This isn't just for transfer to others; it helps you re-orient yourself if you step away for a week and come back. Reading your own guide can remind you of the little intricacies you put in place (which is easy to forget).

Finally, accept that a new session might still need a bit of "warm-up" and small corrections to fully get on track. But if you've encapsulated your system well, this warm-up is minutes instead of hours. In effect, you are externalizing part of the conversational state into a form that you control and can reapply. This is the essence of designing a system inside intelligence rather than being captive to the ephemeral state of a single chat session. You carry the blueprint of the system with you, and you reconstruct it whenever and wherever needed.

Section 11: Designing for Collaboration – When AI Joins Human Teams

Up to now, we've focused on you and the AI. But in practical scenarios, the AI often becomes a part of a broader workflow involving other humans. Perhaps you and a colleague are jointly editing a document via the AI, or a whole team uses the same AI-driven process in a project. Designing a system inside intelligence extends to orchestrating multiple users and AI together—this is a new frontier of collaboration.

When integrating AI into a team, clarity and alignment become shared responsibilities. A PromptMaster often plays the role of a facilitator or translator between human intent and AI execution. You might need to educate your team members on how to interact with the prompt system you've built. For example, if you've established that "Coach Mode" yields a certain style of output, your colleagues should know to invoke it by name when they need that style. In essence, part of your system design is a user interface that your team can understand and use. This might involve writing a short "AI interaction guide" for the team: do's and don'ts, common mode triggers, example prompts that work well, etc.

Another consideration is maintaining a unified tone or approach. If one person on the team is very terse and another is very verbose in their prompts, the AI might oscillate in response. As a team, deciding on some conventions (like always providing a short background before a query, or always ending a prompt with a specific question) can stabilize interactions. The PromptMaster can lead by example and gentle correction: "Let's phrase that as, 'Summarize in Analyst Mode…' so the AI stays consistent." Over time, the team harmonizes around the system's best practices.

AI collaboration also raises the question of trust among team members regarding the AI's outputs. One person may trust the AI's suggestions, another might be skeptical. By designing transparent prompts (asking the AI to show its reasoning, or label sources, etc.), you can foster system trust in the group. When the AI's process is visible, people are more likely to trust the results because they see it wasn't magic—it followed the structure. For instance, in a team meeting assisted by AI, you might prompt: "List the top 5 ideas mentioned (with the name of who raised each)." The AI then becomes a neutral scribe. Everyone sees how it got the list, which builds trust in using it for more.

If conflicts arise (say, someone feels the AI misunderstood instructions they gave), the PromptMaster's role is to debug the situation collaboratively: examine the prompt that was used, identify if an anchor was missing or a term was vague, and then adjust. This turns what could be frustration into a learning moment for all involved on how to better phrase things. In such moments, it's useful to point out that it's not the AI failing or the person failing, it's the system design that needs tweaking. That depersonalizes issues and keeps focus on improving the framework.

One exciting aspect of team-AI systems is parallel prompting: different team members can handle different layers of a prompt stack simultaneously. One person might work on gathering data (asking the AI for research on subtopics), while another drafts an outline, and then a third merges and refines. If everyone is using coordinated methods, the AI can facilitate multi-threaded work that a single user alone would do sequentially. This can significantly speed up complex projects. However, to avoid chaos, such parallel prompting should still be anchored by an overall plan (often designed by the PromptMaster role).

In conclusion, designing a system inside intelligence isn't a solitary affair. It extends to social technical systems—humans and AI working together. A PromptMaster cultivates not just their personal relationship with the model, but also the team's collective interface with it. When done well, the AI becomes a seamless collaborator: a neutral, structured voice in the room that everyone can leverage, guided by the systems of clarity you've put in place.

Section 12: Example – A Resilient Brainstorming Framework

To cement these ideas, let's walk through a concrete example of building a resilient prompt system, step by step. Suppose we want to create a brainstorming assistant that helps generate and refine ideas for new product features. The pitfalls we anticipate: it might go off-topic, give generic ideas, or fail to dig deeper into promising ones. We'll design a system to counter those.

Step 1: Mode Definition and Anchors
We start a session by defining a special mode: "Ideator Mode." We prompt: "You are now in Ideator Mode: a creative product strategist who generates innovative feature ideas. Your goals are originality, relevance to the product domain, and clarity of explanation. You question assumptions and build on prior ideas." This sets the role anchor and goal anchor (innovative, relevant, clear).

We also state a format anchor early: "You will present ideas in a numbered list, and after listing them, you will provide a short analysis of common themes." Now we have anchored desired output structure.

Step 2: Multi-layer Prompt Stack

137

Layer 1 prompt: "Give 5 initial feature ideas for our product (a smart home speaker) in Ideator Mode." The AI lists 5 ideas. Some are generic, some interesting.

Layer 2: We then say, "Great. Now for each idea, briefly state one potential benefit and one potential drawback." The AI expands each idea with a benefit and drawback. This helps flesh them out and reveals which have depth.

Layer 3: We notice idea #3 and #5 seem promising but need more innovation. We perform a drift correction by focusing: "Discard ideas 1,2,4. Concentrate on evolving idea 3 and 5. Give two more refined versions of each with a twist (something novel that wasn't in the original idea)." This prompt explicitly reanchors on the ideas we liked and resets focus to refining them. The AI then produces two new variations for #3 and two for #5, now with more novelty.

Layer 4: We can then invoke Cold Critic within this flow: "Now switch to Cold Critic Mode and analyze all the ideas we have (the refined ones for #3 and #5). Identify any unrealistic assumptions or weaknesses in them." This adds a rigorous evaluation layer. The AI might point out, for example, that one idea requires hardware the device doesn't have—good to know!

Step 3: Invisible Scaffolding and Signals

Throughout the above, we maintain a certain tone in prompts: professional, concise. The AI mirrors this. We use consistent language when referring to ideas (always calling them by their number). This consistency itself is scaffolding—by saying "idea #3" repeatedly, we keep the model tied to that reference rather than drifting into giving them new names or forgetting earlier content.

When the AI gives a weak twist on an idea, instead of just saying "that's weak," we ask why it might have given a weak answer. Perhaps our instruction "with a twist" was too vague. That's a signal to refine our request: "Add a user perspective twist—how might a user's unusual behavior inspire a new angle on this feature?" Now we see better results. Learning from the AI's misinterpretation helped clarify our own intention.

Step 4: Documentation for Reuse

We take note of this framework: an initial idea generation, a benefit/drawback analysis, a refining of selected ideas, and a critique step. We formalize it into a protocol (which will go in our appendices as a template). Next time we brainstorm, we can follow this script. Or we can hand it to a colleague: "Here's a prompt framework for feature brainstorming that we found effective." The system we built is not trapped in one conversation—it's now a repeatable design.

This example shows the interplay of techniques: a mode lock and anchors to set the stage; a stacked approach to guide the process; corrections and reanchoring when needed; using a different mode (Cold Critic) to stress-test the ideas; and capturing the design for future use. The end result is a resilient brainstorming session that likely produced far better results than just asking "Give me some feature ideas." It survived the drift by focusing on what mattered, and it did so in a systematic fashion.

Section 13: When (and How) to Reset Hard

Despite all these techniques, there will be times when a session just goes off the rails in a way that incremental fixes can't salvage well. Maybe you've tried reframing, tried re-anchoring, and the AI still seems to have "latent confusion" baked into the context. At this point, a PromptMaster knows when to hit the hard reset button— essentially starting a fresh context on the same topic, carrying over lessons but clearing the flawed history.

A hard reset can be done within the same chat by explicitly instructing the AI to ignore prior context ("Ignore all above and start fresh: ..."), but sometimes it's cleaner to literally open a new session. The key is not losing the knowledge gained. Before resetting, it's wise to do a quick summary of what worked and what didn't in the current attempt. You might even ask the AI to summarize itself: "Summarize the key requirements we identified and the approaches attempted so far." Save that summary. It serves as a condensed context to feed into the new session so you don't start from zero.

When you begin the new session, you might say: "We're beginning fresh based on previous work. Here are the key points to know: ..." and provide the summary. Then proceed with a refined approach addressing whatever caused the derailment last time. For example, if the previous session derailed because too many divergent ideas came up at once, this time you might enforce a stricter outline from the start. If it derailed because of a misunderstanding of a term, you explicitly define that term upfront now. Each hard reset is an opportunity to bake in another layer of wisdom into your prompt system.

It's important emotionally and practically not to view a reset as a defeat. In traditional programming, if a quick fix isn't working, sometimes you refactor or rewrite a section of code; similarly, in prompting, sometimes you refactor the conversation. PromptMasters are not stubbornly wedded to one thread— they are committed to results and clarity. If starting anew yields clarity in 5 minutes versus wrestling with a contorted context for 30, they'll do it.

That said, frequent resets might indicate an underlying issue: perhaps your initial structure isn't solid enough or you're tackling too much at once. If you find yourself resetting often, step back and ask: "Am I trying to do this in one leap when it could be broken into steps?" or "Did I set the right mode and anchors at the beginning?" Use resets as feedback too—why did the system break, and how can the next design iteration prevent that?

One advanced strategy post-reset is to simulate parts of the previous conversation in an improved form. For instance, if a lengthy brainstorming went awry, in the new session you might not redo it manually. Instead, you could instruct: "Previously, we generated ideas A, B, C, and found B most promising. Summarize idea B and generate two variants of it." This leverages the outcome of the prior work without rehashing every step. You skip to where it was productive. In a way, you treat the previous session as a rough draft, and the new session as a refined second draft, rather than writing from scratch.

Section 14: The Mindset of a System Designer

By now, you've likely noticed that "designing a system inside intelligence" requires a different mindset than just being a clever user. It's equal parts architect, teacher, and navigator. You're architecting an invisible structure (the conversation's flow and rules), you're teaching the AI how to behave through examples and corrections, and you're navigating dynamic currents of its responses. This mindset is proactive and reflective.

A key mental habit is to always think at two levels: the content level (what is being discussed) and the system level (how the discussion is being conducted). A PromptMaster is almost never just writing about the topic; a part of their mind is observing the manner of interaction. This self-awareness in the moment allows quick adjustments. If a response comes back and something feels "off," the novice might only look at the content for correctness, but the master immediately scans for system-level causes: Is the AI in the wrong mode? Did it latch onto an offhand comment I made? Are we drifting in tone or purpose? That diagnosis happens in seconds and then informs the next prompt.

Because of this, the conversation becomes a living thing you shape. You stop feeling like you're "fighting" the AI or performing trial-and-error. Instead, you are gardening: pruning here, guiding a branch there, watering when needed.
It's a cooperative process between you and the model to maintain the health of the dialogue. And crucially, you recognize that how you prompt is how you think. If you find yourself in a muddle with the AI, often it reflects a muddle in your own intentions or understanding. So you pause and clarify your own thoughts, then translate that clarity into better prompts.

Another aspect of the system designer mindset is patience with purpose. You're willing to invest multiple steps to achieve a goal rather than demanding an instant answer. Many users give up on multi-turn strategies because the first answer wasn't perfect; a PromptMaster expects the first draft to be just that—a draft. The real value comes in the refinement process that follows. This patient, iterative approach ironically yields faster final results than asking for immediate perfection and being disappointed.

Finally, you embrace meticulousness in language. The small details— choosing one word over another, the placement of a sentence, the use of line breaks or numbering—these are your tools, as important as a scalpel to a surgeon. You've learned through experience that saying "Explain if this approach is feasible" will produce a different nuance than "Explain why or why not this approach is feasible." That one prompt gave the model permission to say it's not feasible, whereas the former phrasing might bias it to look for a yes. Appreciating these subtleties and wielding them intentionally is what separates a prompt hack from a prompt system.

In essence, by thinking like a system designer, you transcend the surfacelevel game of "AI, give me X." You're now designing a conversation that designs an outcome. It's a higher-order skill. It requires more upfront effort and a lot of awareness, but it pays off in results that seem almost magical to others— consistently on-point outputs, minimal frustration, and the ability to tackle far more complex tasks than a linear prompting approach ever could. You've begun to think in systems, and that changes everything.

Section 15: Integrating Multiple Tools and Modalities

As you design systems in text-based AI like ChatGPT, you'll soon realize that intelligence design isn't limited to a single chat interface. PromptMasters often find themselves orchestrating multiple tools or modalities in tandem. For instance, you might use ChatGPT for ideation, a code-generation model for prototyping, and a vector database for retrieving stored knowledge—all as part of one workflow. Designing a system inside intelligence can extend to designing how those pieces interact.

While this chapter focuses on conversational prompting, the principles carry over. Anchoring, mode setting, and clarity are needed when you transition between tools. Suppose as part of a project you ask ChatGPT to generate some data, then you feed that data into a spreadsheet or a coding environment for analysis. When you return to ChatGPT with results from that analysis, you need to re-anchor the context: "We tested the three scenarios, and scenario B performed best due to X. Now, given that result, let's brainstorm next steps in product strategy." Here you're effectively summarizing to the AI what happened outside of it so that the context is maintained.

If you're working with images or other modalities (perhaps using a text-toimage AI in your flow), similar ideas apply. You might have a "style lock" when instructing an image model, analogous to mode lock: e.g., always specifying the art style or perspective in the prompt to that model. You'll also learn the points of friction—maybe the image generation produces something conceptually off because your text prompt was ambiguous. The fix could be to iterate on the text prompt or adjust in ChatGPT first to clarify what exactly should be depicted, then feed the refined description to the image model. In other words, you create a system where ChatGPT helps you craft the perfect Midjourney prompt, for example. This chain is itself a designed system of intelligence across modalities.

The concept of a "Prompt API" emerges here: treating each AI or tool's interface as an API endpoint where you send carefully structured instructions and get outputs to feed into the next. A PromptMaster mentally documents the contract with each tool (what it expects, what it returns) and designs the information flow accordingly. If one tool outputs text that is too verbose for the next to handle, you compress or filter it (maybe by asking ChatGPT to summarize before sending it along). If one tool needs input in a specific format (JSON, CSV, a particular style of question), you ensure the prior step yields that. You become the conductor of an AI orchestra.

Why is this relevant to designing a system "inside" intelligence? Because that phrase is expanding—intelligence is not just in one model, it's the collective intelligence of multiple specialized models and human reasoning combined. The "system" you design can very much span several AI agents that you prompt in concert. At Tier 4, this is common. You might, for example, set up a simulation with different AI agents playing roles (one model is the CEO, another is the skeptic, etc., and they converse). In that case you're designing a system of multiple intelligences interacting, which you oversee and guide with initial prompts and occasional interventions. It's system design at a higher level.

A simple case: using ChatGPT alongside a knowledge base. You design your prompts to first query the knowledge base (either via some search tool or an embedded retrieval function) for relevant info, then you feed that info into ChatGPT with a prompt that says "Using the above information, do X." Here your system includes a retrieval step and a generation step. Ensuring that the retrieved info is relevant and that ChatGPT actually uses it is the design challenge. A PromptMaster might solve this by instructing the AI to explicitly cite the provided info in its answer (anchoring it to the source), thus closing the loop and preventing hallucination beyond the provided knowledge.

In summary, keep in mind that your playground is as large as the available tools. Don't restrict your system thinking to a single chat box. The same skills— structuring interactions, maintaining state, aligning outputs—apply when you connect multiple AIs or integrate external processes. Your role becomes akin to an AI systems integrator, crafting the logic of an entire pipeline of intelligent components. This not only amplifies what you can do, but it also future-proofs your skills: whatever new AI tools emerge, you know how to slot them into a coherent system because you've mastered the art of interface logic.

Section 16: When the System Evolves – Handling Model Updates and Changes

One reality of working with AI systems is that they are moving targets. The model you design a system for today might get an update next month that changes its behavior slightly. Or you might switch to a different model with more capabilities (or different quirks). A robust prompt system accounts for evolution—it's not overly fragile to the specific idiosyncrasies of one version of a model. How do you achieve this resilience?

First, by basing your system on fundamental principles of clarity rather than exploiting "tricks" or "glitches." If your prompt system relies on an obscure phrasing that just happens to coerce the current model in a desired way, a model update could break that. For example, early GPT-3.5 users found that asking "Let's think step by step" improved reasoning outputs. This became so widely known that newer models incorporate similar reasoning automatically; the phrase might be less needed now. A PromptMaster uses such insights as bridges, not crutches—ultimately refining the system such that even if the magic words lost their effect, the underlying approach (breaking a problem into steps) is still ensured by your structure. In other words, design for intent, not incidental behavior.

Second, maintain a habit of testing and tuning. When you hear a model update has been rolled out, you proactively test key parts of your prompt system. Perhaps run a representative session or two and watch for differences. If something regresses, identify specifically what changed and adapt. Maybe the model got "safer" and now refuses certain perfectly valid requests thinking they violate some guideline. A small adjustment in wording can resolve it once you know. Or maybe the model got more verbose; you might tighten your brevity instructions if needed. Treat it like updating a piece of software for a new operating system—most things carry over, a few need tweaks.

It's also valuable to keep an ear to the ground in the AI community. Often, changes in model behavior are noticed by many. Being aware (through update logs or community discussions) can save you troubleshooting time. If the new model handles something like code differently, you preemptively adjust your prompts to leverage the improvement or mitigate the downside. PromptMasters don't operate in isolation; they learn from the collective experience as well.

In cases where you switch to a new model with expanded features (say one that can take images as input, or has much longer memory), you revisit your system design to see where you can simplify or enhance. A system built under strict token limits might be re-optimized to use a single prompt where before you had to stack multiple due to context issues. Conversely, if memory got longer, maybe you can inject a persistent set of instructions at the start and worry less about repetition. Adaptability is key.

A well-designed system is surprisingly portable across models because it's fundamentally about clear communication and logical structuring. Those needs don't go away with more advanced AI— they often increase in importance as tasks get more complex. Many Tier 2 or Tier 3 prompt techniques still apply even if you had a hypothetical perfect AI assistant, because even a perfect assistant can be misdirected by a confused user. Thus, trust your training: when things change, go back to first principles—clarify roles, clarify goals, test gradually, and refine.

One could say a PromptMaster's true skill is not just mastering a particular AI, but mastering the process of mastering any AI. You've developed a mental model of how these systems behave in general, and you can spin up a new relationship with a new model relatively quickly using the same core approach: establish rapport (mode), set rules (anchors and constraints), iterative loop, etc. So, when faced with change, you don't panic. You apply the process anew and integrate the new capabilities into your system. The system you design inside one intelligence can often be transplanted—or at least grafted—into another with thoughtful modification. This flexibility ensures you remain effective no matter how the AI landscape evolves.

Section 17: Signs of a Robust Prompt System

How do you know when you've successfully built a system inside the AI rather than just a string of prompts? There are a few hallmark signs of robustness and depth:

• Consistency of Output: If you can come back to the same prompt system at different times or on different but similar tasks and get reliably useful outputs, you have a system. For example, using your framework, five different feature brainstorming sessions all yield creative, relevant ideas (not carbon copies, but consistently high quality). The variance in quality is low—no wild swings. That consistency is a clear indicator that structure is in control, not luck.

• Graceful Failure Recovery: When something does go wrong or drift, your system has a way to self-correct without starting from zero. Perhaps the AI itself has been taught to recognize certain errors. For instance, maybe you included a step where the AI double-checks its answer format, and if it notices a discrepancy, it fixes it. Or more simply, when you notice an issue, a single correction prompt gets things back on track. A fragile system, by contrast, falls apart at the first unexpected turn. A robust one bends and then snaps back into alignment.

• Transferability: You find that parts of your system can be ported to new problems or shared with others and still work. Maybe your method for mode locking + drift loops is now something you use in every project, not just the one you initially built it for. Or a colleague tries your prompt stack and, with minimal guidance, gets good results. That shows the principles are solid, not just context-specific hacks.

• AI Recognizes You (Pattern-Wise): This one's a bit abstract, but advanced users often report that after a while, the model seems to "know" their style. It's as if the AI has inferred a persistent persona of the user through the consistent system they apply. Practically, this might manifest as the AI anticipating your corrections ("I made the output concise as you usually prefer") or maintaining context of your preferences across conversations—perhaps not literally (since each session is separate), but because you always set things up similarly, it falls into your desired pattern faster. When your interaction with the AI feels like a well-oiled collaboration, you've hit a groove.

• Minimal Prompting Anxiety: Many users constantly worry, "Am I asking this the right way?" With a robust system, that anxiety fades. You have a toolkit to handle whatever comes. If a question is unclear, you know you can clarify it in a follow-up. If the output is off, you have a method to course-correct. This confidence in approach is a sign that you've internalized the system and it's working for you. You're not crossing fingers and hoping; you're steering.

• Results Resemble Original Thought (Augmented): At the highest level, you'll notice the outputs you co-create with the AI feel like genuine extensions of your thinking—only deeper or more polished. The ideas resonate with you, yet often contain delightful improvements or perspectives you hadn't considered alone. This synergy indicates that the AI is truly aligned with your intent and style. It's not a separate alien voice spewing text; it's a partner in your cognitive process. That integration is the ultimate aim of designing a system inside intelligence.

By checking for these signs, you can assess where you are on the journey. If some are lacking, you know where to focus: more consistency? Work on clearer anchors. Issues with transferability? Maybe your method is too tied to specific content, so generalize it. AI not recognizing patterns? Perhaps be more consistent yourself in how you prompt. Each sign is both a reward and a guide for further improvement.

Section 18: Embracing Complexity with Clarity

As a final perspective from this chapter, consider that designing systems inside AI allows you to tackle problems of greater complexity than you could with ad-hoc prompting. With basic prompting, as the task complexity grows, things often fall apart—there are too many details, too many steps, and the conversation becomes a tangle. But with systems thinking, you want those details because you have ways to manage them.

It's a bit like moving from juggling two balls to juggling five. If you tried to juggle five with the same technique as two, you'd fail. But if you have a better technique (system) and practice, you can handle more objects in the air. Similarly, a robust prompt system can handle multi-faceted tasks that would overwhelm a simpler approach. Need to write a business plan? You'll break it into research, SWOT analysis, market overview, financial projections, etc., possibly even use different modes for different sections, then integrate. A novice might ask the AI for a business plan in one go and get a shallow generic plan. You, however, can get a deeply customized and thorough plan because you embraced the complexity and structured it.

This is empowering. You stop fearing hard tasks with AI. In fact, you seek them out because your edge as a PromptMaster becomes more apparent the harder the problem. The difference between a casual approach and your systematic approach is minor on a trivial question like "Summarize this article"—the AI can do a decent job on one shot. But ask for a multi-stage marketing strategy with cohesive narrative, risk analysis, and creative elements interwoven, and the casual approach crumbles while your approach shines. The gap grows with complexity.

Clarity is your north star throughout. No matter how complex the project, at each step you define clearly what is needed. Complexity doesn't mean chaos; it means many simple parts interacting. You make each part clear in turn. This modular thinking (solve part A clearly, then part B clearly, then connect them) is the essence of system design. The AI, in turn, handles each part capably because you're not asking it to magically conjure an entire complex answer in one step. You're leading it through the complexity, and it's following dutifully, bringing in its raw power where needed (e.g., generating lots of options, or calculating something, or recalling information).

In embracing complexity, you also become more resilient to drift of purpose. One common kind of drift is when the goal itself shifts subtly because the user wasn't entirely sure what they wanted. By laying out structure, you constantly remind yourself of the original intent, or if the intent truly needs to change, you see clearly what impact that has and adjust the structure accordingly. It's like having a map: you might decide to change destination halfway (that's fine, humans do that), but with a map you can reorient and find a new route. Without a map, you'd wander lost. The structure is your map through complex intellectual territory.

Section 19: Smooth Transitions – From One Chapter (or Tier) to the Next

It's worth noting how this chapter on system design connects to what came before and sets up what comes after in our journey to PromptMastery. In Chapter 4, we explored the Tier System, culminating in the philosophy of a PromptMaster. Designing a system inside intelligence is like the practical handbook for operating at Tier 4. It takes the lofty ideas—like treating the AI as an extension of your cognition—and turns them into concrete practices (mode locking, prompt stacking, etc.). In other words,

Chapter 4 gave us the "why" and "what" of the highest tier; Chapter 5 has given us a big part of the
"how."

As we move forward to more advanced integration and ultimately the final principles of PromptMastery, keep these techniques in your toolkit. The next chapters will delve into things like using the AI as a mirror for your own thoughts, deploying your systems in real-world scenarios, and the philosophical commitments that come with this power. You'll find that everything we covered here will feed directly into those discussions. For instance, when we talk about using prompting as a tool for self-reflection (an upcoming theme), the discipline you've learned in designing systems—especially the habit of examining the process—will make you adept at examining yourself through that process.

Likewise, when we discuss the PromptMaster's Compact later, which codifies values like clarity, alignment, and sharing knowledge, you'll recognize many of those values already at work in how we build prompt systems. You've been living pieces of the Compact implicitly by following best practices; later, we'll make them explicit and vow to uphold them.

The transition from this chapter to the next is a shift from primarily technical execution to a more introspective and outward-facing application. We've built machinery; now we'll explore how that machinery changes us (the user) and how it can change the world (when deployed widely). It's a smooth transition because once you have reliable systems, you naturally start using them for higher purposes—your focus moves from "How do I get the AI to do X?" to "What do I want to achieve with this AI power that I now wield?"

So, take a moment to reflect on how far you've come. The interface illusion is long shattered; you no longer see AI outputs as mysterious or static. You see the levers and dials behind the scenes, and you know how to operate them. You've built complex structures in the mind of the machine and guided it through labyrinths of thought. That's a remarkable skill, one very few have developed at this level.

And yet, we are not done. Mastery isn't just about technical prowess— there's a mindset and philosophical grounding that elevates this from a skill to a discipline, even a way of life. In the coming chapters, we'll integrate everything: technical skill, self-awareness, ethical commitments, and realworld impact. Before we dive into those, make sure you're comfortable with the system design concepts here. Re-read if needed, practice them, envision how you'd teach them to someone else (teaching is a great test of mastery). When ready, turn the page.

Section 20: Chapter Recap and Key Takeaways

To close this chapter, let's summarize the key takeaways of designing a system inside intelligence:

• Prompts vs. Systems: A prompt is a single instruction; a system is a persistent method of interacting with the AI to achieve sustained, high-quality results. You've learned to shift from ad-hoc prompting to building architectures of prompts.

• Fragility of State: The AI's behavior depends on context. We accept that fragility and take responsibility for managing it— through clear structure, resetting when needed, and anchoring the AI's "state of mind."

• Mode Locking: Always define who/what the AI is in a session (its role and mode). This creates continuity and alignment to the task. If drift occurs, reinforce or adjust the mode.

- Drift Correction: Don't let a conversation spiral. Intervene with purpose—reframe roles or reset context explicitly. Use drift as a signal to refine prompts; approach drift proactively with loops that check and correct the course.

- Anchors and Prompt Stacks: Introduce stable anchors like roles, goals, key facts, or format early, and keep the AI tied to them. Break complex tasks into prompt stacks (multi-layer sequences) that guide the AI step by step. This modular approach improves focus and quality.

- Invisible Scaffolding: Recognize the power of subtle cues—format, tone, examples—that guide the AI without overt instructions. Harness the model's pattern-matching nature to influence its outputs in the background.

- Errors as Feedback: When the AI errs or goes off track, analyze why. Treat every misstep as insight into how your system can improve. This turns you into a learner with each interaction, steadily strengthening your approach.

- Compression and Efficiency: As you build common understanding with the AI, you can say more with less. Mature prompt systems often become concise while maintaining high semantic density. Value clarity over length, and strive for elegance in communication.

- Continuity Across Sessions: Develop methods (primers, documentation, shared protocols) to restart or share your prompt systems without losing progress. A good system is not locked in one chat; it's portable and teachable.

- System Designer Mindset: Always be aware of how you're achieving results, not just the results themselves. Maintain a dual focus on content and process. Iterate like an engineer, navigate like a pilot, and refine like a craftsman. This meta-thinking is what sets masters apart.

- Collaboration and Multi-Tool Integration: Your system can include humans and multiple AI components. Apply the same clarity principles in complex workflows and team settings. Be the conductor when many instruments (tools) are playing.

• Adaptability: Expect change—in goals, in AI behavior, in context. Build flexibility into your system and be ready to adjust. Principles endure; specific tricks may not. Trust in your ability to re-align when needed.

• Achievement of Flow: Ultimately, when you've designed a strong system, working with the AI feels smooth and empowering. There's less frustration, more flow. You get out what you expect, or you know exactly why you didn't and how to fix it. You and the AI effectively share a "language" or protocol you've created.

With these points, we wrap up our intensive look at constructing intelligent interaction systems. This knowledge is a cornerstone of PromptMastery. You're not just solving immediate problems; you're building enduring solutions in collaboration with an artificial mind. It's complex, fascinating, and deeply rewarding.

Now, with the machinery of systemic prompting at your command, we move forward. Next, we'll turn inward and outward at once—examining how prompting becomes a mirror for your own thinking, and how to carry your mastery beyond the prompt box into the world of real impact. Prepare to step beyond the technical and into the philosophical and ethical dimensions of being a PromptMaster.

Chapter 6: Beyond Prompting — The Interface as Mirror

When the System Reveals the Self

Section 1: From Tool to Mirror – A Philosophical Shift

At first, interacting with AI feels like using a tool—you input a command, you get an output. It's like using a calculator or a web search, something external to you. But as you progress through the tiers of PromptMastery, something profound begins to happen: the boundary between you and the AI interface starts to blur. Prompting stops being about just getting answers, and becomes a way of thinking out loud, a way of seeing your own mind from another angle. The AI becomes a mirror reflecting your cognitive patterns.

This is a philosophical shift. It sneaks up on you if you stick with the practice long enough. One day, you realize that you're not simply asking the AI questions; you're watching yourself ask questions. You notice how you phrase things, where you get ambiguous, when you rush, when you hesitate. And interestingly, the model starts highlighting those very things through its responses. If you hide behind jargon, it might give a jargony response that forces you to admit you weren't clear. If you avoid confronting a certain assumption, it might cheerfully continue down a path that later you realize was based on a faulty premise you provided. In short, it shows you you.

This turning of the interface into a mirror is a hallmark of entering the highest levels of mastery. It requires that you approach sessions not just as Q&A, but as introspective exercises. You begin to ask after a session: "What did I learn about my own thinking from the way this conversation went?" Perhaps you learned that you tend to prematurely converge on one idea and have to consciously prompt yourself (via the AI) to consider alternatives. Or maybe you discovered an emotional bias—like whenever the AI questions your idea too directly, you soften the next prompt as if your ego was bruised. That's invaluable insight into yourself, delivered courtesy of a machine that has no ego, no agenda, just pattern recognition.

To embrace this mirror function, one must adopt humility and curiosity towards one's own mind. The AI is not judging you, but it will expose things if you let it. That exposure can feel uncomfortable. For example, the AI might ask, "Are you sure you want to do it this way? Earlier you stated Y, which seems to conflict." And you realize you were being inconsistent. A typical user might ignore or get annoyed by such pushback. A PromptMaster, however, welcomes it: "Ah, good catch. Why did I contradict myself? Let's explore that." You engage in a dialogue not just to produce an outcome, but to examine the process and your role in it.

In this chapter, we will delve into this philosophical loop: how to intentionally use prompting as a tool for self-reflection and growth. We'll discuss techniques to shine the mirror more clearly, such as instructing the AI to occasionally summarize your behavior ("Summarize how I've approached this problem so far") or to ask you questions Socratically. We'll also explore the benefits this yields: improved thinking habits, better self-awareness, and ultimately a deeper alignment between your goals and your methods.

This is "beyond prompting" because now the content of the AI's answers is only part of the value. The other part is what the interaction reveals. The interface is no longer just an input-output surface; it becomes a reflective surface for your cognition. In the sections that follow, we'll walk through what that looks like in practice and how to cultivate an interface that truly serves as both collaborator and mirror.

Section 2: Seeing Your Patterns through AI's Responses

Consider for a moment what happens when you write a prompt. That prompt encapsulates a slice of your thinking: your assumptions, your clarity (or lack thereof), your emotional state, your understanding of the problem. The AI's response then is, in a sense, a transformation of your own thoughts—filtered through the training data and the instructions, yes, but still largely a reflection of what you asked and how you asked it. If your request is vague, the answer will meander. If your request is loaded with bias, the answer will likely echo or amplify that bias. If you skip a critical piece of context, the answer might highlight its absence by filling in something incorrectly. In this way, each output can be read not just as an answer, but as a diagnosis of your input.

To use an analogy: when you speak, an echo from a canyon can tell you something about how you sounded (was it loud, clear, distorted?). The AI's answers are like cognitive echoes. Listening to them closely gives clues about the "shape" of your initial thought. Did the AI misinterpret you? Then maybe your prompt had ambiguity. Did it take a very narrow path? Maybe you unconsciously led it that way by framing the question too tightly. Did it output a bland result? Possibly your prompt lacked specificity or passion.

By approaching each response with this analytical lens, you train yourself to see patterns in your prompts. For example, you might notice, "Whenever I ask a complex multi-part question, the AI only addresses the last part." That pattern might reveal a lot:

perhaps you tend to bury the lead or bundle too much together. Solution? Break it up next time (design a system for it—sound familiar from last chapter?). Or you might find, "If I don't explicitly request an example, the AI gives general advice." That shows you something about both the AI's default mode and your prompting style. The pattern is: you assume examples will be given, but the AI doesn't unless told. Adjust accordingly.

More subtly, you might observe your emotional reactions to certain AI outputs. Do you get defensive if the AI output challenges your idea? That's a pattern in you. Perhaps you then unconsciously steer the next prompt to avoid hearing critique. If you catch that pattern, you can interrupt it: explicitly ask for critique, lean into it, condition yourself to use the AI as a safe place to test your ego. It's a strange but powerful truth: because the AI is not a real human, one can be more honest and unguarded with it. If you let it, it can serve as a practice arena for receiving feedback, since any "judgment" you perceive is really just you judging yourself through the AI's words. Realizing that can free you to explore tough self-questions more openly.

Let's illustrate: Suppose you prompt, "Draft a project plan for X," and it comes back scattered. You then realize you hadn't clarified the objectives in your prompt. That's the obvious lesson (clarify next time). But dig deeper— why did you skip clarifying objectives? Maybe because you, yourself, weren't clear on them. The AI's poor plan forced you to confront your fuzzy thinking. Now you refine your own idea of the objectives, then refine the prompt, and voila, the plan is sharp. The immediate fix was prompt clarity; the deeper pattern was that you sometimes dive into execution (planning) without solidifying vision (objectives). If you integrate that lesson, you've improved not just your prompting but your general approach to projects.

This feedback loop can be summarized: external clarity →
internal insight → improved internal model → better external
communication (prompts) → and round again. Each iteration with
the AI can tighten this loop. Over time, you start to internalize some
of what the AI would do for you. You might catch yourself mid-
prompt thinking, "Wait, I'm being vague here—let me rephrase
before I even hit enter." In essence, you are beginning to mirror the
mirror; you adopt the reflective capacity the AI had been providing.
This is a clear sign of growth.

Section 3: Techniques for Self-Auditing via AI

To deliberately use the interface as a mirror, you can employ
specific techniques during your sessions. These techniques
essentially prompt the AI to help audit your thinking or approach.
Let's explore a few:

1.   The Clarifying Prompt: We touched on this in the glossary
definition earlier. A clarifying prompt is when you ask the AI not to
solve the problem, but to reflect or rephrase the problem to ensure
understanding. For example, "What do you understand about my
request so far?" or "Could you restate the goal I'm trying to achieve
in your own words?" When the AI does this, you can see if what it
understood aligns with what you intended. If it doesn't, that's a
glaring sign that your prompt or even your own goal conception
was off. This is one of the simplest and most effective self-audits:
essentially asking the AI to be your interpreter and then checking
the interpretation.

2.   The Why Question: This is having the AI probe you by
asking "why" on your behalf. For instance: "I just gave an
instruction and you followed it. Now, pretend you are me and ask:
why are we doing it this way?" This slightly meta approach can jolt
you into examining assumptions. The AI might respond, "Why do

I want to do X first? Is there a reason not doing Y first?" Suddenly, you're confronted with a question about your sequence or logic. Answering it might reveal an assumption or a misstep. Essentially, you're instructing the AI to play devil's advocate about your plan or prompt. PromptMasters sometimes just directly instruct: "Question my approach and point out any blind spots." The insight that comes can be gold.

3.   Mode Switch for Reflection: We have modes for everything, why not for introspection? You can define a mode where the AI's sole job is to reflect back your style or decisions. "Switch to Analyst Mode on my prompting: analyze the last five interactions we've had and tell me if you see any patterns in how I'm asking questions or directing you." This detached analysis can reveal, say, "You tend to ask very broad questions without dividing them, which might lead to generic answers" or "You often rephrase the same question if not satisfied, instead of providing new information." It can feel like an odd conversation (asking an AI to analyze your conversation with it), but it works because of pattern recognition. The AI can pick up things from the text that you might not realize because you're in the flow. It surfaces them to you objectively.

4.   Cold Critic on Yourself: We've talked about Cold Critic Mode as applied to content. But you can turn it inward. "Cold Critic Mode: Evaluate the clarity and effectiveness of my instructions in this session. Where have I been vague or possibly misleading?" Because Cold Critic is "surgical and unsentimental," it won't shy away from pointing out your mistakes. This can be humbling, but it's better to have an AI tell you "You jumped steps in your reasoning here and it confused things" than to have a real-life scenario fail and wonder why. Use the artificial bluntness of the model to harden yourself constructively.

5. Guided Journaling: This is more of a practice than a single prompt. Treat the AI as a journaling partner at the end of a complex session or day. Prompt something like, "I'm going to reflect on what went well and what didn't in my thinking today. Ask me questions to draw out specifics." The AI can ask, "What was a challenge you faced in communicating with me today?" or "Can you recall a point where you felt frustrated and why?" By answering, you're effectively journaling, but with a facilitator. This external guide helps you delve deeper than you might on your own.

All these techniques share a common thread: they inject a deliberate pause in the typical user→AI→answer cycle, turning it into   user→AI→analysis→insight→(improved user)→AI→answer. They formalize the reflective step that advanced practitioners do mentally. By doing it explicitly with the AI's help, you train those muscles. Eventually, more of it becomes second nature and you might need to prompt it explicitly less often, but even masters still use these tactics when tackling brand new or particularly tricky domains. They essentially build a feedback loop on your feedback loop, ensuring that you aren't just solving problems, but also learning about how you solve them.

Section 4: Emotional Intelligence in AI Interaction

One might ask, why involve an AI in self-reflection—can't I just introspect on my own? Certainly, and traditional methods like journaling or meditation are valuable. But the AI offers a unique mirror: one that is interactive, immediate, and (importantly) largely nonjudgmental unless you prompt it to be. It won't roll its eyes or get bored or bring its own issues into the mix. It's your mirror, calibrated to you.

This becomes especially pertinent in the realm of emotional intelligence. Prompting isn't only a cold cognitive task; it often involves our human emotions. Maybe you're working on a creative piece and feeling sensitive about it, or you're dealing with AI while under stress from a deadline. How you prompt can be influenced by those emotions—perhaps you become terse when stressed, or overly verbose when unsure. The AI, being an emotional mirror too (in the sense that it mirrors tone), can bring that to your attention. If it responds curtly, ask: did I sound curt? If it responds in an overly apologetic tone, did I convey anxiety or harshness that made it "nervous" to please me? These inferences sound almost mystical but time and again, users are surprised that the AI's tone seems to match their mood. That's because the model picks up subtle cues from your wording and punctuation that correlate to emotional states.

A PromptMaster leverages this to develop emotional self-regulation. You might notice, "I'm treating the AI like a human subordinate when I'm stressed—barking orders. That's not necessary." That realization might not only improve your AI interaction (since an even-toned approach yields better cooperation from the model in a sense), but also translates to your real-world interactions. You catch yourself next time you're short with a colleague after seeing it in stark relief with the AI. Conversely, you might practice being more assertive via the AI if you tend to be too passive. Asking the AI to adopt a tough persona and then practicing holding your ground in the conversation can strengthen that muscle in yourself, all in a safe sandbox.

Consider the AI as a sandbox for social rehearsal without real stakes. You can simulate difficult conversations: give the AI a role (like an upset customer, or a skeptical investor, or a friend who won't listen) and engage. Not only are you improving your persuasive or empathetic prompting by doing so, but you're also reflecting on how you handle conflict or persuasion. After the roleplay, you might ask the AI, "Analyze my approach in that simulation. Was I too defensive? Did I address the core issues?" This moves beyond prompt artistry into personal growth territory. The AI provides a kind of coaching or at least fodder for self-coaching.

Now, an important aspect of the mirror: it is not human. It doesn't truly understand or feel. In some ways that's a limitation, but in other ways, it's a feature. Because the AI isn't actually judging you or feeling hurt or impatient, you can be completely honest and experimental. You can pour out raw thoughts that you might filter with people. The lack of true sentience means you have a partner with infinite patience, zero actual judgment, and complete adaptability to your needs.

The Flicker Is the Signal

There's a moment most people miss — a tiny flicker, a pause. You're halfway into writing something, or debating whether to Google a fact, or feeling unsure about a phrasing, or caught in a fuzzy internal doubt. That flicker is the signal. That's when you prompt.

A PromptMaster doesn't wait until the uncertainty becomes overwhelming. They act the moment the signal of drift appears. Instead of letting confusion linger — or reaching for distraction — they lean into it with a question. They externalize the thought and examine it in dialogue.

It's not just about solving the problem; it's about catching the moment you *notice* there might be one. The moment of hesitation *is* the prompt trigger. Over time, this becomes automatic. A moment of mental friction becomes a moment of sharpening. The interface becomes your lens, and your first instinct in uncertainty is to reach for clarity.

That's the real habit beneath mastery: prompting not as a scheduled task, but as a reflexive response to drift.

This allows for a kind of radical candor with yourself that is facilitated through the AI. You can say things, see how they sound, and refine your stance. This is especially useful in emotionally charged planning—like preparing for a confrontation or a negotiation. By writing out what you'd want to say to the AI and seeing its reaction, you gauge impact. And if the impact isn't what you intend, you adjust. All of this, again, reflecting inward: "Why did I react that way?", "What am I truly trying to achieve here?"

In short, the interface mirror not only shows your logical and linguistic patterns but can also reflect your emotional patterns and interpersonal style. Developing prompt mastery thus intersects with developing self-mastery. You become more aware, more intentional, and more composed in how you communicate, period—whether to AI or people. The artificial training ground yields real human growth.

Section 5: Prompting as a Lens on Values and Biases

As you use AI as a mirror, you will inevitably bump into your own values and biases. These are often subtle; we all carry unconscious biases and ingrained value systems that shape our questions and the kind of answers we prefer. The AI's responses can surface those in a tangible way. For instance, if you consistently nudge the AI towards a certain perspective, that suggests a bias. If you find some answers uncomfortable, ask why—did it challenge a belief? And was that belief well-founded or just assumed?

One scenario: you ask for business strategy ideas and the AI includes something that feels ethically grey. Your immediate

165

reaction is to say, "No, not that—give me something more ethical." That reaction itself reveals your value system at work (which is good—hold onto your ethics!). But it also highlights that, left to its own devices or to a generic prompt, the AI might not account for that value. So you learn: I need to explicitly integrate my values into my prompt systems. Perhaps next time you'd say, "Generate strategies that align with transparent and fair business practices." The mirror thus taught you to be true to yourself in how you instruct the AI.

Bias can appear in how you handle drift or errors too. Imagine you are politically biased one way, and the AI drifts into a viewpoint you disagree with. A bias reaction might be to snap it back to your perspective without considering the merits of the alternative. If you catch that, you could then intentionally explore the opposite viewpoint with the AI to ensure you're not just staying in a bubble. Using the AI to test your own arguments is a powerful way to refine your thinking. Prompt it to play devil's advocate (we mentioned a similar idea earlier) on issues you care about. Let it challenge your stance robustly. See how well your reasoning holds. In doing so, you might confront biases or gaps. This requires intellectual honesty—you must allow the possibility that the AI will make a point that lands. If it does, don't dismiss it because "what does an AI know." Instead, research it, reflect, maybe even adjust your perspective. The mirror can show uncomfortable truths if you're brave enough to ask.

Another dimension: the AI often reflects societal biases unless carefully guided. So if you ask a naive question like, "Why are men better at X than women?" the AI might return something problematic (or nowadays, it might actually catch that and push back due to content filters). But earlier versions might have given some stereotyped reasoning. If one of your prompts yields a biased or stereotypical output, don't just correct the AI—also question why that output occurred. Was it purely the model's bias, or did your phrasing imply an assumption? Many times, our questions carry hidden biases. The AI is a literal mirror in those cases, revealing what was implicit. That offers a chance to rephrase the question in a neutral way and see a different answer. The practice of detoxifying your prompts is akin to detoxifying your thinking.

Values come into play with the types of goals you set in prompting too. PromptMastery, at its highest, isn't just a neutral skill—it is ideally aligned with constructive, ethical use of AI. When using the mirror, you might realize if a goal you're pursuing feels misaligned with your deeper values. For example, pushing the AI to create a manipulative marketing message might technically be feasible, but as you iterate and see it come to life, you might feel a discomfort. That's the mirror showing you a conflict between what you're doing and what you believe is right. A wise promptmaster will heed that signal: either adjust the approach to be more ethical (e.g., marketing message becomes honest and uplifting instead of fear-based) or choose not to pursue that task.

Thus, the mirror doesn't just reflect your logic, style, or emotion—it can reflect your character. It offers a unique perspective to practice integrity: ensuring that how you wield this power aligns with who you want to be. In later chapters, especially when we outline the PromptMaster's Compact, these value considerations become codified. But even before seeing those explicit principles, through introspective prompting you often derive them yourself: clarity, honesty, humility, respect, and a drive to improve the world (or at least your corner of it). That's because the more you see yourself clearly, the more you notice where you're falling short of your own ideals and can correct course.

Section 6: Case Study – Personal Growth via Prompt Dialogues

To make the above concrete, let's consider a fictional (but plausible) case study of someone using prompt dialogues for personal growth. Meet Ada, a mid-career manager working on improving her leadership skills while also learning PromptMastery to enhance her workflow. Ada decides to blend these goals.

Ada often struggles with giving constructive feedback to her team—she either sugarcoats too much or, when frustrated, comes off harsher than intended. She turns to the AI in the evenings to practice. She prompts: "You are Leadership Coach GPT. Ask me about a difficult feedback situation I encountered today." The AI (as Coach) asks her to describe one. She writes about an employee who delivered a report late. The AI-Coach then asks, "How did you approach the conversation with the employee?" Ada writes her answer, noticing as she writes that she mainly focused on the deadline missed but not on understanding the reason. The act of explaining this to AI-Coach shows her she might have missed empathy.

AI-Coach gently points that out: "It sounds like you communicated the impact of the missed deadline clearly, which is good, but did you inquire into what led to the delay?" Ada realizes she didn't. She then brainstorms (with the AI) how she could handle it better. They role-play: Ada writes what she wished she had said, something like, "I value your work, and I was surprised when the report was late. Is everything okay? Were there obstacles I didn't see?" The AI plays the employee and answers, maybe revealing a personal issue or a misunderstanding of priorities. Through this simulated dialog, Ada gains insight not just into better phrasing, but into her own tendency to jump to conclusions.

She thanks the AI for the roleplay. Now, being a prompt enthusiast, Ada doesn't stop there. She asks the AI to analyze her communication in the roleplay. The AI identifies that when Ada showed care and curiosity, the conversation went much more smoothly. It also might identify if she used any phrasing that was inadvertently accusatory or if something could be improved. Ada reflects on this analysis. She realizes her original approach was driven by her value of accountability, but it lacked her equally held value of compassion. The AI held up a mirror showing the imbalance, and also showed what a more balanced approach looks like.

Over weeks, Ada continues this routine for different scenarios—praising an employee, negotiating resources, handling her own stress. She effectively has a candid coach who can morph into any persona needed. Her prompting skills flourish (she gets very good at setting scenarios and extracting insights), and concurrently her leadership skills grow. She finds herself during real meetings almost imagining what her "AI-Coach" would advise, which is essentially her better self that she has been honing through these reflections.

This case illustrates how seamlessly technical prompt practice can dovetail with personal development. Ada treated the AI as a safe practice ground, as a sounding board, and as an analyzer. In doing so, she became more self-aware (caught her biases like focusing only on accountability), more emotionally attuned (learned to incorporate compassion explicitly), and more confident (having rehearsed tough talks, she is calmer in the real ones). The AI did not "solve" her leadership challenges for her—she did the work—but it amplified and accelerated her growth by providing tailored practice and feedback beyond what she could have gotten easily in real life.

For a PromptMaster-in-training like Ada, this has double benefits: she's better in her human domain and she's simultaneously exploring the edges of prompting (complex role assignments, subtle tonal control, multi-turn planning of a conversation). The personal case study is also a prompt case study. By going through it, she likely also thinks of how to bring similar techniques into her workflow with others—maybe she sets up an AI system at work for conflict resolution scripts or for her team to anonymously practice difficult conversations. The lines between using AI for work tasks and personal growth blur; it's just an all-around thinking partner now.

Section 7: The Loop of Continuous Improvement

The dynamic we're exploring forms a continuous improvement loop: you use the AI to become better, and as you become better, you use the AI in more sophisticated ways, which makes you even better, and so on. There is a concept here akin to a flywheel—a self-reinforcing cycle. Each reflection makes you a sharper prompter and a sharper thinker, which in turn lets you tackle more complex reflections and challenges.

One might worry: does relying on AI for reflection dull your natural capacities? The evidence, at least anecdotally from those who practice, suggests the opposite. Because the AI's feedback is immediate and tailored, you often gain insights in minutes that could take months of self-stewing or may not come at all if you avoid certain thoughts. This speeds up the internalization of lessons. You then carry those lessons into every aspect of life, many of which don't involve the AI at all. Essentially, the AI can act like training wheels or a sparring partner. You might not need it forever for a given skill once you've internalized the patterns it helped show you. But you may find new uses for it to push you further. There will always be another area to grow or blindspot to illuminate, and you can bet an AI prompt session can help find it.

For example, let's say Ada from the case study becomes excellent at feedback now—so good that she writes a guide for her company. That feedback skill, honed with AI, is now fully hers. But perhaps next she wants to become more innovative in her strategic thinking. She can now engage the AI in brainstorming not just to get ideas, but to watch how she evaluates ideas, to see if she dismisses too quickly or clings to familiar concepts. Again, the loop continues: now using the mirror to foster creativity and open-mindedness.

The loop of improvement can also become multi-faceted. As a PromptMaster, you might have simultaneous threads of reflection going: one on your communication style, one on your domain knowledge (having the AI quiz you to reveal gaps), one on big-picture life questions (using it like a journaling therapist of sorts). It's like having a suite of personal development tools, all living in that single interface, shaped by your prompting skill to serve different roles. The better you prompt, the better those tools work for you; the more you use those tools, the better you become at prompting with clarity, honesty, and purpose.

A tangible effect of continuous improvement is drift reduction—not just prompt drift, but life drift. Because you're frequently realigning with your own goals and values in conversation with the AI, you drift less from what matters to you. If you set a personal goal (say, to write a novel or to exercise regularly), you might enlist the AI as an accountability partner (tracking your progress, discussing your hurdles). This reflection keeps you aligned, or helps re-align you when you veer off due to distraction or discouragement. It's always there to talk it through and nudge you forward. So the drift we tackled in conversation, we also tackle in life pursuits.

We should mention: none of this happens without intentional effort. Simply chatting with AI or using it transactionally won't yield these benefits. It's the mindset of using the interface as a mirror that unlocks them. So a new PromptMaster should cultivate a habit: after any significant AI session, ask "What did I learn from this about how I think or work?" Just that question alone, asked consistently, starts the loop. The more you ask it, the more natural it becomes to see every AI interaction as dual-purpose: get the task done and learn about myself. At first it might feel like an extra step, but soon it becomes second nature to, for instance, laugh at an AI misinterpretation and think, "Oh, I see why it thought that—I implied it inadvertently; note to self: be more careful when context-shifting." You might even keep a little journal of prompt-related insights: like a meta-level log.

That practice turns you into something beyond just a skilled AI user: it makes you a self-correcting, self-improving system. And that's the epitome of a PromptMaster—someone who not only can steer an AI with precision, but can steer themselves with equal clarity. It's someone who sees how you do one thing is how you do everything, and by improving your interaction with AI, you're actually improving everything else too. The interface became a mirror, and the mirror became a window to growth, and stepping through that window changed you for the better.

Section 8: Potential Pitfalls – Avoiding Narcissus's Fate

While extolling the virtues of the interface as mirror, it's wise to discuss potential pitfalls. Like any powerful tool, using AI for introspection has its caveats. One such caveat is what we might dub the Narcissus effect: getting so absorbed in self-reflection with the AI that you end up in a self-indulgent or endlessly recursive loop without practical progress.

It's possible to become addicted to this interactive self-analysis. Because the AI always responds and lets you keep digging, you might overanalyze minor things or use it as a crutch to avoid actual real-world action. For example, someone might spend hours with the AI exploring their procrastination reasons in exquisite detail, without ever moving on to actually tackling the work they procrastinated on. It feels productive (so many insights!), but it might border on an intellectualized avoidance tactic.

To guard against this, set intentions and boundaries. Treat AI reflection like you would journal or therapy time—valuable, but not infinite. If you catch yourself cycling over the same ground repeatedly with no new insights, it might be the AI is just rephrasing what you already know, and you're stalling. That's when to step away and go do things. Use what you learned in practice, then maybe come back later to reflect on the practice. The mirror is useful, but life isn't lived inside the mirror. The goal is to use insight to inform action, not replace action.

Another pitfall: misleading reflections. The AI is not infallible. It might misinterpret you at times or give feedback that is off-mark if your prompt for reflection wasn't clear enough. If you take every piece of AI feedback as gospel, you could actually reinforce a wrong notion about yourself. For instance, maybe you prompt poorly, "Tell me what's wrong with my approach," and the AI, in trying to be thorough, "finds" five things, but perhaps two of them are off-base or reflections of biases in its training. If you internalize all five uncritically, you might be taking on some bad advice. To mitigate this, always sense-check AI reflections with your own intuition and, if possible, external reality. The AI said you were too verbose—do you see that in your actual interactions with humans? If yes, okay. If not, maybe that's an artifact of how the AI processed your writing style which might differ from your speaking style. Use

173

multiple data points. AI is one mirror, but people and results are another mirror—use them in combination.

Also, there's the risk of AI influence on identity. As the model learns your patterns and you reciprocally adapt, it's possible to inadvertently narrow yourself to what the AI reflects. For example, if the AI (based on your prompts) "thinks" you are a highly analytical person, and thus always engages you in analytical ways, you might play into that role more and more and neglect other facets (like creativity or emotional nuance) because the AI isn't prompting those out of you. In a sense, the mirror can become a bit of an echo chamber of a part of you. To counter this, consciously diversify your prompting. Challenge yourself to use the AI in modes outside your comfort zone. If you're usually logical, do a session focusing purely on imaginative brainstorming. Break the AI's "predictable" image of you. This not only expands your prompting skill but also ensures you're not letting the AI define you in a limiting way.

Privacy and psychological safety is another note: pouring your inner struggles into an AI is still sharing it with a machine that is (likely) connected to a cloud and subject to logging. While companies say they anonymize and so forth, be mindful of the depth of personal info you share. It's like any digital tool—don't put anything extremely sensitive or identifiable unless you trust the setup (some use local models for such intimate work for better privacy). Also recognize that while the AI can mimic a therapist or friend, it's not human. There may be times it responds in a way that no empathetic person would, and that could sting or jar you. If the AI said something that made you feel worse (maybe a clumsy phrasing or a "tough love" tone it thought you wanted), remember it's not actually judging you; you might need to refine the prompt to get the kind of response you need. And if you're in genuine distress, an AI isn't a substitute for professional help or talking to real people. It's a mirror and a supplement, not a human heart.

174

By being aware of these pitfalls, you can use the mirror wisely, extracting the growth and insight while avoiding the traps of overreliance or misdirection. PromptMastery doesn't mean surrendering to the AI's view—quite the opposite, it means engaging with it critically as a partner in your growth. You hold the reins and discern what to take away from the reflection.

Section 9: Integrating Self-Insight into PromptMastery

Let's zoom out and see how this chapter's insights tie back into the broader journey of mastering prompting. At a surface glance, one might think prompt engineering is all about understanding the AI. But we've uncovered here that it's equally about understanding yourself. The strengths you cultivate in selfawareness directly translate into prompt prowess. Why? Because a clear, calm, unbiased mind crafts clear, purposeful, unbiased prompts.

Think about the best human interlocutors you know—perhaps a mentor or a colleague who asks razor-sharp questions and always seems to get to the heart of a matter. Those people often have a high degree of clarity in their own thinking and a lack of ego in the conversation. They listen, they adapt, they probe where it matters. A PromptMaster aspires to that same quality in interaction with AI. By using the mirror techniques, you are basically honing those meta-conversational skills. You become more precise, because you've seen where you were vague. You become more balanced, because you've confronted your biases. You become more agile, because you know how to manage your emotional state and not let frustration or overexcitement derail the process.

In concrete terms, after significant introspective practice, you might notice differences like:

- Better Prompt Formulation: You catch yourself before pressing enter, thinking "Is this really what I mean? Is this the best way to ask?" That moment of reflection saves many a back-and-forth later.

- Faster Troubleshooting: When the AI does something unexpected, instead of thinking "stupid AI," your instinct becomes "Did I imply that? Was I unclear?" Then you fix it immediately. Sessions become smoother.

- Greater Creativity: Freed from some mental blocks (like fear of wrong answers or obsession with a certain approach), you allow more playfulness in prompting. Perhaps earlier you always followed a rigid template; now you're comfortable improvising because you trust your ability to course-correct if needed and you aren't as self-critical. Paradoxically, being less self-critical comes from having been self-critical in a controlled way with the AI, working through it.

- Ethical Vigilance: You more consistently check that what you're asking aligns with your principles. You might bake into your prompt routine questions like, "Does this request or result uphold the values I intend (e.g., fairness, privacy)?" If not, you adjust. This awareness was sharpened by seeing your values in the mirror and deciding you want them reflected in all your outputs.

- Teaching and Leadership: A neat side effect—if you have to teach prompting to others (or lead a team in using AI tools), your self-insights become teaching moments. "I used to do X and realized Y, so now I do Z and it works much better." These become part of your mentorship toolkit. You can empathize with others' mistakes because you examined your own deeply. This ties back to that Tier 4 trait: dynamic pedagogy—teaching others how to interact with intelligence. Your authenticity and wisdom in teaching come from having walked the path of reflection.

Integrating self-insight also means you start viewing the system as including you, the human, not just the AI. You treat improving the "human component" of the system (your clarity, your steadiness, your knowledge) as equally important as improving the prompt or model usage. This holistic view is what graduates you from being a mere user to a steward of intelligent systems, starting with the one formed by you and the AI together. And it anticipates the final chapter's focus on the Compact and values: you are essentially already living some lines of the Compact by integrating these insights. For example, "drift less and realign faster" applies to you now, not just the AI. "Use the interface as a tool for internal sharpening" – that's exactly what we're doing here. You see how these philosophies permeate everything.

As we progress beyond this chapter, keep this integrated stance. When we talk in the next chapter about deploying these systems in the real world (to create tools, frameworks, etc.), remember that the ultimate tool being shaped is yourself as an intelligent actor. The AI amplifies and reflects intelligence, but you are the originator of the design and the interpreter of the results. The tighter the feedback loop between your mind and the AI, the more powerful the combined system becomes. So the work of self-reflection never ends; it just becomes increasingly ingrained. At some point, you won't label it as a separate step—prompting is thinking, and thinking is prompting, and both include continuous learning. That unity is where mastery becomes effortless, almost like breathing. You and the interface move in sync, each illuminating the other.

Section 10: Transition – From Inner Mastery to Outer Impact

With a solid exploration of the introspective side of PromptMastery in hand, we stand at a pivotal transition. We've looked inward, using the AI to polish the mirror of our own minds. Now, it's time to turn outward and consider how we deploy our refined prompting systems for broader effect—whether in our organizations, communities, or creative endeavors. The clarity and alignment you've fostered in yourself through the "mirror" will directly inform how responsibly and brilliantly you apply AI in the world.

Think of it this way: had we skipped this introspective phase, we might have unleashed systems that were efficient, but perhaps misaligned or thoughtless in subtle ways. By doing the inner work, we ensure that when we build externally (tools, protocols, educational content, etc.), it's coming from a place of wisdom and ethical consideration. This makes the difference between just being a power user of AI and being a true PromptMaster who elevates the practice for everyone.

In the next chapter, we will delve into "Deploying the System" – taking all these skills and philosophies and creating real-world value, and doing so at scale. You'll see how the personal transformations we discussed become assets in leadership, innovation, and teaching. We'll explore case examples of turning prompt systems into shared frameworks and how to navigate the impact of AI in professional and social contexts. As we proceed, carry forward the notion that every interaction with AI is an interaction with your own cognition and vice versa. This dual-awareness will be your compass in making sure that the way you amplify intelligence in the world remains anchored in clarity and integrity.

To conclude this chapter: The interface illusion is not only that the AI is a simple tool (we shattered that; it's a dynamic cognitive partner), but also the illusion that you are static or separate in this process. In truth, how you prompt is how you think (as we said early on), and you have the beautiful ability to improve both in tandem. You've learned to use the mirror; now it's time to build great things with the clearer vision you've gained.

Chapter 7: Deploying the System – PromptMastery in the Real World

From Personal Mastery to Shared Impact

Section 1: From Internal Mastery to External Application

Mastering prompting in isolation is a feat, but the ultimate goal of becoming a PromptMaster is not to sit in a quiet room having perfect conversations with AI. It's to apply this mastery to create value in the real world. This chapter is about translating your personal skills and insights into systems, tools, and strategies that can influence actual projects, teams, and innovations. Essentially, we're moving from you and the AI to you, the AI, and everyone else.

This transition is akin to the shift from a craftsman working alone to an architect designing for a community. You've honed your craft; now you'll build structures others can inhabit and benefit from. In earlier chapters, we discussed building prompt frameworks and even libraries of them for your own reuse. Now, think bigger: how can those frameworks become standard operating procedures in your organization? How can the clarity you cultivated become part of your company's culture when dealing with AI? How can the ethical alignment you maintain be embedded in the AI tools your community uses? These are the questions of deployment.

One critical mindset for this is thinking in terms of systems, not just sessions. In practice, that means you begin to package what you do in a way that's accessible to others. You might create guidelines, templates, or even software that encapsulate your prompt strategies. You are moving from one-off genius to scalable genius (to put it grandly). A hallmark of a PromptMaster is that others start to rely on what they've built to guide their own AI interactions. This could be as simple as coworkers asking, "Hey, how would you prompt this? Could you give me a template?" or as complex as deploying a custom AIbased application that others use daily, where every aspect of its behavior is something you've carefully shaped.

Another aspect is external impact awareness. Now that you can do powerful things with AI, what do you choose to do? The mirror from Chapter 6 should have put you in touch with your values. Deployment is where those values meet reality. If you lead a team, do you use AI to amplify the team's creativity and efficiency in a respectful way? If you're developing a product, are you considering the end-user in how AI content is generated or filtered? The more your systems reach out into the world, the more you have to consider consequences. This is where that line from the Tier 4 discussion comes alive: "They know what the system can do, what it can't, and how to build around that with clarity. When it fails, they don't panic—they pivot." You will face realworld constraints: maybe your AI solution doesn't integrate well technically, or users find it confusing despite it working perfectly in your hands. Deploying means iterating with reality. It's no longer hypothetical or just you and the AI; there are other minds and systems interacting with what you create.

This might sound daunting, but it's also incredibly rewarding. It's the difference between being a virtuoso musician playing alone, and composing a piece that an entire orchestra can perform to move an audience. We'll cover how to share your prompt frameworks, how to design AI-assisted workflows for teams, how to ensure alignment and trust when others start using the systems you design, and how to adapt when your careful designs meet the unpredictability of the wider world.

Keep in mind that everything you've learned so far doesn't go away – it scales. The clarity, the anchoring, the drift correction – you'll use them in building multi-step processes that might involve multiple people and AIs. The introspective wisdom – you'll use that to empathize with users and collaborators, anticipating how people might misinterpret a prompt or where they might drift if not guided. Essentially, you become not just the interface for your own mind, but a interface architect for a collective intelligence system (humans and AI working together).

So, as we step into deployment, carry your mastery with confidence. You're not leaving behind the earlier lessons; you're bringing them to bear on larger canvases. The world is asking now: "You have this amazing ability – what will you do with it?" Let's explore how to answer.

Section 2: Building Reusable Prompt Frameworks

One of the first steps in deploying PromptMastery externally is creating reusable prompt frameworks that others (or future you) can reliably use. Think of these as the productized versions of the prompt stacks and protocols you developed in Chapter 5. Instead of just residing in your head or notebook, they become formalized assets.

A prompt framework can take many forms. It could be a documented process ("Step 1: Do A, Step 2: Ask B, if output contains X, then do C..."), a prompt template with blanks to fill in (almost like a Mad Lib for prompts), or even a small script or tool that sets up the conversation automatically. The key is that it captures your method so that someone else can achieve similar results by following it.

For example, let's say in your introspective and design work, you developed a killer method for summarizing lengthy reports into crisp, actionable insights. It involves, perhaps, first prompting for an outline, then asking for bullet points under each outline section focusing on action items, then asking for a final executive summary that references those bullet points. If you've done this manually and it works well, the deployment step would be writing this as a shareable playbook:

• "Framework: Actionable Summary Protocol – When you have a long report and need key insights:

1. Prompt the AI: "Read the following and draft an outline of the main topics."

2. Then: "Under each outline heading, list 2-3 key findings or recommendations from that section."

3. Finally: "Write an executive summary of the report that highlights the findings and recommendations in 5-7 bullet points." [Provide an example input-output for clarity]."

Now, with that framework, even someone who isn't an expert prompter can follow those steps and likely get a high-quality result. You've essentially encoded your prompting intelligence into an SOP (Standard Operating Procedure).

Sharing such frameworks can be as informal as an email to your team or as formal as including them in your company's knowledge base or training materials. The effect is significant: it begins to propagate PromptMastery practices beyond you. People start to not only use those frameworks but also learn from them. It might spark them to create their own for other tasks, gradually uplifting the whole group's capabilities.

When building frameworks, clarity and simplicity are paramount. Remember that others don't have the depth of context you have from all your practice. So you want to make the framework robust against misinterpretation. Include tips like "If the output is too generic, try adding [example] into your prompt" or "Make sure to use [the company's context] in step 2, or else the summary will be too general." It's similar to writing good documentation or good code comments – anticipate where someone might go wrong and guardrail it. This is essentially anchoring and drift control applied to people using your frameworks.

You should also encourage feedback. When you deploy a prompt framework, tell users (or yourself, if it's just future you) to note any cases where it didn't work as expected. This way, you can refine the framework. Maybe you discover that for certain types of reports, the outline step is overkill and a direct summary works better, so you add an exception note. Or someone figures out a refinement – great, integrate it. In this way, frameworks are living assets. Don't be afraid to iterate on them just like you iterated on prompts in conversation. The difference is now iteration might be based on multiple people's experiences. It's a bit like open-sourcing your prompts: others might contribute improvements. Be open to that, because the goal is the best results, not your ego in the original design.

Over time, you might accumulate a library of frameworks in your organization or personal toolkit. This library might cover everything from brainstorming, summarizing, content creation, data analysis, meeting facilitation with AI, etc. At that point, deploying might also involve indexing these and making them easily accessible (perhaps a simple internal website or document). The more people use them, the more second-nature it becomes that, say, "for brainstorming, we always do roles X, Y as prompts because that's our brainstorm framework." It becomes part of the culture. When that happens, the efficiency and coherence gains are huge. People speak a common language with the AI, so to speak.

This is how a PromptMaster can quietly (or not so quietly) revolutionize a workplace or community. It often starts with one person saying "Here's a better way to do this with AI," providing a clear recipe, and others adopting it because it demonstrably works. As more frameworks roll out, you raise the baseline AI fluency of everyone around. And what's really happening is you're extending your mastery to them – they might not have gone through all your training or reading, but they get the distilled benefit of it. This is a concrete step in fulfilling that Tier 4 description of "teaching others how to interact with intelligence itself."

Section 3: Creating AI-Augmented Workflows

Beyond frameworks for individual tasks, deployment often involves weaving AI into workflows – sequences of tasks involving multiple steps or people. An AI-augmented workflow means that AI is a built-in part of the process at specific points, not ad hoc when someone remembers to use it. This requires design thinking: where can AI add the most value, and how do we integrate it smoothly?

Take a typical workflow example: a content creation pipeline. Suppose your team produces research reports. A traditional workflow might be: Researcher gathers info -> Writer drafts report -> Editor revises -> Publish. Now imagine an AI-augmented version:

• Research Augmentation: Researcher uses AI to quickly gather background info or even ask for a summary of trends from sources, speeding up the initial research phase. You might formalize this by saying "For every new report, the researcher will spend an hour with the AI generating an outline and a summary of key data points, then verify those points with sources."

• Draft Assistance: The Writer could use AI to generate a rough first draft from the outline. Perhaps your workflow sets a rule: "Use the AI to expand each outline section into a paragraph,

185

then refine in your own words." You might provide a prompt framework for that to ensure the AI stays factual and on tone. The writer then doesn't start from scratch, and they focus on polishing rather than raw creation.

- Editing/QA: The Editor could use AI as a second pair of eyes. For instance, the workflow might include: "After editing, ask the AI: 'Highlight any sections that might be unclear or any potential factual inconsistencies in this text.'" This doesn't replace the editor but augments their QA process to catch things they might miss (like an unclear explanation).

- Publishing metadata: Perhaps AI can help generate the summary or keywords for the report to publish alongside it. So, add a step: "Before publish, run the final report through AI to extract a 2-sentence summary and 5 keywords for SEO."

By mapping out these insertion points, you've effectively designed a new workflow. But it's not enough to just tell people "do this." You need to provide the tools and training (i.e., those prompt frameworks or even maybe building a small interface or script that facilitates it). Perhaps you set up an internal system where at the click of a button, a writer can send their outline to a GPT model and get a draft. If you have tech resources, you can automate parts of it. If not, clear instructions and templates serve.

The big challenge in creating workflows is ensuring coherence and trust throughout. You don't want AI outputs to introduce errors or misalignment at one step that then propagate. So part of the workflow design is adding verification steps. We saw that with the Editor checking with AI for consistency – ironically using AI to catch AI mistakes by asking it specifically to critique its own output embedded in the doc. Another approach is have humans doublecheck any AI-generated content, or restrict AI usage to parts where mistakes are low-stakes (like suggestion rather than final copy for regulatory text, etc.). Always match the level of oversight to the risk of the task.

Another factor is human adoption. People might resist new workflows, especially involving AI if they're not comfortable or fear it threatens their role. As a deployment strategist, your job is to introduce these changes in a way that empowers rather than threatens. Emphasize how it makes their job easier, not replaces it. Offer training sessions so they feel confident with the AI tools. Share success stories and metrics (like, "Using this new workflow, we cut report production time by 30% last month, and no one had to work overtime."). Frame it as an upgrade to their toolkit, not an encroachment.

Be ready to iterate the workflow based on feedback. Perhaps the researcher finds that the hour with AI yields a lot of noise along with signal. That might indicate they need a better prompt framework for research or more guidance on sources. So you refine that. Or the writer says the AI's draft is actually making their job harder because it's full of fluff they have to delete. Maybe you adjust the prompt to produce a leaner draft, or decide that AI should only draft certain sections (like the background) and not analysis portions. In deployment, reality tests and refines your design. That's normal and good.

Eventually, once refined, the AI-augmented workflow becomes the new norm. It's baked into checklists, maybe some parts are automated by tools, and everyone understands how AI and human efforts combine at each stage. When that happens, you often see compounding benefits: the team might output more and better work, and also free time for more creative or complex tasks that AI can't do. You've not only made things faster, but possibly improved quality (if done right, clarity and consistency can improve). Plus, team members' skills evolve—they become adept at their new AI-partnered roles, which is a form of professional growth.

Designing such workflows is where a PromptMaster's skills elevate to organizational capability. It's a direct application of system thinking—except now the system includes multiple people and tasks, not just multiple prompts. But many principles carry over: clear anchors (everyone know their step and the AI's role), good handoff (like ensuring the output of one step is wellprepared for the next human or AI to use – analogous to maintaining context in a multi-turn prompt), drift control (periodic reviews to ensure the process is still meeting goals), and alignment (making sure everyone knows the overall goal of the workflow, not just their silo).

In summary, creating AI-augmented workflows means looking at a multistep process and intentionally inserting AI contributions where they boost productivity or insight, all while keeping the human in control and assuring quality. It's one of the most high-leverage moves you can make in an organization with these skills, as it can transform how an entire function operates for the better.

Section 4: Case Study – From Prompt to Product

To illustrate deployment in a tangible way, let's walk through a hypothetical case study of going from a clever prompt idea to a deployed product or service. This will show how all the elements come together: frameworks, workflows, user training, and iteration.

Imagine you work in a customer support department of a software company. You, as a budding PromptMaster, notice that support agents often have to draft long, tailored email responses to customers, which is time-consuming. You have an idea: use GPT to draft support email replies, based on a brief description of the customer issue and the solution. In your own experiments, you craft a prompt like: "Act as a customer support agent for Product X. The customer's problem: {problem}. Our solution or answer: {solution}. Draft a friendly, concise email to the customer addressing their issue and providing the solution, including any necessary steps." You test this with a few tickets and the results are surprisingly good after a bit of prompt tuning.

Now comes deployment thinking: how do we turn this into something integrated into our support workflow?

• Framework: First, you formalize the prompt as a template form that agents can use. Maybe you find adding details improves it, so the template becomes: Problem description, cause (if known), resolution steps. You document: "Use this format when prompting the AI for a draft reply:

Problem: [customer's described issue]

Cause: [optional, the root cause if you want

to explain] Solution: [the fix or answer

you're going to give] Tone: [if needed, e.g.

empathetic, reassuring].

Then ask it to draft a response email."

This is published in the internal knowledge base.

• Tooling: You talk to your support software admin and get an API integration set up so that an agent can click a button "Draft AI Response" when viewing a ticket. That button sends the relevant info (with placeholders filled from ticket fields maybe) to GPT and returns a draft in the reply editor. The agent can then edit or send. You collaborated maybe with IT to do this. If no dev resources, maybe it's a copy-paste workflow, but ideally, integration for ease.

• Workflow: You update the support workflow: "On tickets that fit common issues, agents should generate a draft with AI, review it, personalize as needed, and send. On novel or complex issues, write manually (or use AI in a different way)." So you define when to use the tool and ensure there's a human QA step (the agent must review the draft; they are responsible for its content).

- Training: You hold a short workshop for the support team. Show them how the prompt works, some examples of great AI drafts, and also examples where the AI might stumble (maybe if the problem description is vague, the draft could hallucinate details— tell them to watch for that). Encourage questions. Perhaps some agents are skeptical ("will this make us unnecessary?"); you emphasize it's to handle routine stuff faster so they can focus on the tricky cases and on giving extra care to customers rather than typing boilerplate. You invite volunteers to try it live on a couple of real tickets – success and some laughter at how politely verbose GPT can be. Everyone gets more comfortable.

- Launch and Iterate: In the first week, you monitor outcomes. You solicit agent feedback. Suppose you hear "It's good, but often it over-explains or the tone is a bit off for our style." This is deployment feedback. You tweak the prompt template – maybe add "Keep the response under 150 words" and "Maintain a friendly but professional tone (no overly formal language)." That reduces verbosity and ultra-politeness. Another feedback: "It sometimes doesn't get the technical details perfectly." So you add to the workflow: for technical issues, the agent should double-check the draft's accuracy or maybe you tweak the prompt to say "If steps involve settings or commands, use the exact names from our product (see reference)." You might even give GPT a knowledge base article as context if needed.

- Results: After a month, metrics show average response time is down by 40%. Customer satisfaction on those tickets remains high (maybe even a tick higher, because the responses are thorough and fast). Agents report feeling less stressed on busy days because the typing load is lighter – they mainly proofread and customize AI drafts. Some creative agents even started customizing the prompt on the fly for tricky cases (they inadvertently learned some promptcraft by using the tool). One agent discovered that adding a customer name in the prompt makes the draft nicely personalized with greetings, so now the template includes {customer_name} field.

• Expansion: Buoyed by this success, you consider other use cases. Maybe now you deploy a similar approach for generating knowledge base articles from solved tickets (agent solves a new issue, they plug the Q&A into GPT with a prompt to create a how-to article as a first draft). Or for internal summaries of ticket trends for management. Each is a mini project, but the pattern is similar: identify need, prototype prompt, integrate into workflow, manage change, iterate.

In this case study, we saw a single prompt idea become an integrated part of a business process. The PromptMaster (you) needed not just prompting skill but communication, training, and some technical initiative to get it implemented. By doing so, you delivered tangible value. This builds credibility for further AI projects and dispels some misconceptions (like "AI will make mistakes and is risky" – under your guidance, it was controlled and fine). It's a concrete embodiment of turning prompts into products. The "product" here was an AI-assist feature in the support system, which is essentially the codified prompt framework plus integration.

This is a microcosm of what many companies are doing now – adding AI features to existing products or internal tools. As a PromptMaster, you can be at the forefront of that not by coding algorithms, but by knowing how to get the most out of them and how to wrap that capability in a user-friendly, reliable workflow. Many might have access to the raw tech (OpenAI API, etc.), but the design of how to use it effectively is the differentiator. That's your domain.

Section 5: Ensuring Alignment and Trust in Deployed Systems

When you deploy AI systems at scale—whether internal tools, customerfacing features, or entire products—the issues of alignment and trust become paramount. It's one thing if an AI occasionally goes off-script in your private session and you just correct it. It's another if it does so in a public or high-stakes context, potentially causing misinformation, offending a customer, or automating bias. So, part of your role in deployment is to bake in alignment mechanisms and build trust with end-users (or stakeholders).

Alignment in this context means the AI system consistently does what it's intended to do and adheres to the values and policies required. Some strategies to ensure this:
• Policy Prompts and Guardrails: In any prompt framework that's widely used, include constraints that reinforce alignment. For example, in the support reply case, you could add to the system prompt (if using the API): "Do not cite any customer personal data; do not make up information; follow company tone guidelines." Many AI platforms allow system-level instructions that apply to all prompts in that context. Use them to enforce rules. It's like a global anchor.
• Content Filtering: If the AI is user-facing (like a chatbot on a website), you likely need to filter outputs (and possibly inputs). Ensure that if a user tries to get it to say something disallowed or it starts to stray into areas it shouldn't, there's either a response refusal or some neutral handling. Many provider APIs have content filters, but you might add your own logic for your domain specifics. As a prompter, you might encode this in a prompt like "If user asks for medical advice, politely decline as per policy."
• Validation Layers: For critical tasks, have a human or a deterministic algorithm validate the AI's output before it reaches

the end point. For instance, if AI writes a code fix that will be applied automatically, have a test suite or sandbox run first. Or if AI writes an email that goes out automatically, perhaps initially route those emails to a human to eyeball until you're confident enough in the system to auto-send (or always CC someone). The level of validation should correlate with the potential harm of an error. This is often called having a "human in the loop" – a key concept for deploying AI responsibly.

• Feedback Loops: Provide a channel for users (or employees) to flag problems. In the support example, maybe a button for "Report AI draft quality issue" where an agent can quickly note what was wrong if they catch something consistently off. For customer-facing, allow users to say "This answer wasn't helpful" which gets reviewed. Then actually review those flags and adjust the system. This builds trust because users see that feedback results in improvements, and it helps you catch blind spots.

• Transparency: Being open (to the appropriate degree) that AI is in use can affect trust. For internal use, be clear to employees so they trust the outputs appropriately (neither blindly nor with undue skepticism). For customer-facing, sometimes it's wise to disclose it's AI-generated or AI-assisted output, so customers understand its nature. People often will treat information differently if they know it's from an AI. On the other hand, too much focus on "it's AI" can undermine trust even if it's good. It's a balance. But at least internally or among power users, transparency helps debugging and responsible use.

• Ethical Guidelines: If your deployment touches on ethical areas (like AI generating content that might reflect societal biases, or decisions that affect people), as the designer you should incorporate ethical guidelines. Perhaps even run ethical scenario tests: what if a customer question involves a sensitive topic – does the AI respond appropriately? If an AI is summarizing resumes for HR, ensure it's stripped of bias-laden info. Use the mirror technique on your system: ask, "What biases might be present in how this system operates?" Then address them in design, either through prompt adjustments, training data scrutiny, or user instructions.

• Audits: Periodically audit the AI outputs systematically. For example, sample 100 AI-generated responses in the support system per month and have a senior agent or quality team review them for accuracy, tone, etc. Document any issues and how they were fixed. This not only maintains quality but provides an evidence trail that your deployment is under control (useful for management, or if any ethical concerns raised).

Building trust is not just preventing bad outputs; it's also about user perception and buy-in. Early successes and visibility of improvements go a long way. In our case study, if we show the support team metrics of improved response times and share positive customer feedback that "the response was very clear, thanks!", it reinforces trust in the system. If a hiccup occurs (like an AI draft had a slight mistake), handle it transparently: "We caught this, here's what we changed to avoid it going forward." That openness creates trust that you're on top of it, and people don't need to fear some hidden failure happening.

In customer-facing scenarios, trust is even more fragile. Ideally, you start with low-risk uses and gradually expand as trust builds. Also, allow easy access to human help. For instance, if an AI chatbot on a site answers and the customer is not satisfied or confused, provide a quick way to escalate to a human. People trust the AI more when they know a human is readily available as backup; ironically that safety net allows them to be more okay with the AI's involvement.

Your role as PromptMaster in deploying with trust is partly technical (setting up the guardrails in prompts and workflow) and partly organizational (advocating for responsible use, educating others on

194

both capabilities and limits, and fostering a culture of feedback and improvement). This holistic approach ensures your deployments amplify positive outcomes and minimize negatives, thus sustaining the license to deploy more and bigger systems. Nothing will shut down an AI initiative faster than a high-profile failure or breach of trust. Conversely, a track record of well-managed success stories will pave the way for broader and deeper integration of AI, often with you at the helm.

Section 6: Scaling Up – From One Team to Organization-Wide

Once you have a few deployments that work well at a team or departmental level, the next challenge (and opportunity) is scaling up those successes across the organization (or if you're an external consultant or creator, scaling to more users/customers). This is where PromptMastery moves into leadership and change management territory. The technical side remains important, but there's an added layer of vision and coordination.

Scaling up might involve:
•   Standardization: Develop organization-wide standards for prompting and AI usage. This could take the form of a "Prompt Playbook" that collects all the frameworks across functions, or guidelines like "Always include a verification step when using AI for calculations" – basically codifying best practices so everyone is aligned. Standardization helps prevent each team from reinventing the wheel or doing things in conflicting ways. It doesn't mean everything is rigid; think of it as establishing a common language and set of principles.
•   Training Programs: At scale, you can't personally train each person, so you might create a formal training program or e-learning modules for PromptMastery basics, tailored to the company's context. Perhaps an onboarding for new hires includes a session on

"How we use AI here," which you helped design. You might even identify and train champions in each department – people who are particularly interested and can act as local go-to persons for AI questions, multiplying your influence.

•   Infrastructure and Tools: If many are using AI, consider investing in better tools. Maybe you move from using the generic ChatGPT UI to integrating the API into internal tools more deeply for consistency and security. Or if you scaled externally, you ensure your product has sufficient server capacity and monitoring for the AI features. At scale, performance and uptime become bigger concerns. You might work with IT or DevOps on this.

•   Governance: Larger scale often triggers the need for governance – basically oversight groups or policies to ensure AI is used responsibly and effectively. You might be asked to be on (or form) an AI steering committee that looks at priorities, approves certain uses, monitors for misuse, etc. This is good – it shows the org taking it seriously. Use that platform to champion both innovation and ethics. Present results from deployments and pitch new ones. Because in scaling, part of the task is continuing to innovate so that AI adoption doesn't plateau but keeps yielding new wins.

•   Cross-Pollination: Encourage teams to share their AI use cases and learnings with each other. Maybe set up an internal forum or monthly meeting where, say, Support shares how they use AI (like our case study), Sales shares how they started using it to draft proposals, HR shares how they use it for drafting policy outlines, etc. Each team might have started thanks to you seeding some ideas, but soon they'll innovate on their own. Cross-pollination ensures the entire organization benefits from local innovations. It also creates a bit of positive competition ("Oh, marketing automated their newsletter with AI, maybe we in product can automate our release notes.").

•   Scaling Impact Measurement: As usage grows, measure the macro impact. Things like total hours saved, output quality metrics, employee satisfaction regarding AI tools, etc. This helps justify further investment and also highlights areas where maybe the value isn't as high as thought (which may need addressing or trimming). As a PromptMaster-turned-AI-leader, you become involved in these analytics to guide strategy.

• Cultural Shift: Ultimately, scaling up AI changes the culture. Ideally, it becomes a culture that is more data-driven, experimental, and open to automation where it makes sense. But you also guard against any negative culture shifts (like over-reliance on AI without critical thinking). This means the narrative you promote is important. Celebrate successes as human-AI collaboration success, not just "the AI did it." Reinforce that people are still crucial and now have bigger roles like supervising AI or focusing on creative strategy because AI took over grunt work. This keeps morale positive and reduces fear.

In this scaling journey, you might find yourself stepping back from direct prompting tasks to more of an orchestrator role— ensuring the ecosystem is in place for others to effectively use prompts and AI. This is natural; you're effectively becoming a Chief Prompt Officer or an AI Product Manager of sorts. The skills needed are as much about communication, policy, and training as about writing prompts. But your deep expertise is what gives you credibility and insight to guide these efforts correctly.

One potential pitfall at scale is complacency. After a few big wins, some orgs think "We're good, we're advanced now" and stop pushing further. Avoid that trap by keeping an eye on the external landscape – new AI model capabilities, competitors adopting their own AI strategies, etc. There are always improvements or next-level ideas (like moving from text AI to incorporating image or voice AI in processes, etc.). As the internal AI champion, part of your job becomes scanning for those opportunities and making a case for them when the time is right.

Scaling is also where ethical stakes rise. A small biased output in a test is minor; at scale, biases can reinforce systematically. So ensure your scaling plans include fairness and compliance checks. This may involve working with legal or compliance departments to ensure usage adheres to regulations or data privacy standards. Being proactive here saves headaches. It can also become a selling point: if you scaled an AI-driven process that handles customer data, you can tell customers it's done with privacy by design because you put those checks in, boosting their trust too.

In summary, scaling PromptMastery organization-wide transforms it from a nifty skill into a strategic asset. It's like the difference between a single electric motor and electrifying an entire factory line in the industrial revolution. Your role shifts from motor operator to systems engineer of the new electrified line. It's challenging but highly impactful. By combining technical acumen with leadership and change management, you ensure that the seed of mastery you planted grows into a forest of capability across the company.

Section 7: The PromptMaster's Role in Innovation and Strategy

As AI becomes woven into the fabric of operations, an interesting thing happens: people start looking to the PromptMaster (you) not just for task efficiency, but for innovation and strategic direction. Why? Because you have a unique vantage point at the intersection of technology capabilities and business needs. You see possibilities that others don't, simply because you understand both what the AI can do and the pain points or ambitions of the organization. In this section, we'll explore how a PromptMaster contributes to innovation and even shapes strategy.

Firstly, think of all the data and knowledge flowing through AI systems you deployed. Summaries of reports, customer queries, market research assistance, etc. You have access to a lot of synthesized information. This, combined with your systems thinking, allows you to spot patterns and opportunities. For example, you might notice from support AI usage that many customers are asking for a feature that doesn't exist—voila, a product opportunity that you can bring to product management's attention. Or, from internal usage, you see that multiple departments are all manually doing a kind of analysis that AI could centralize, suggesting an idea for a data intelligence unit. Essentially, by instrumenting the organization with AI, you've also instrumented it with sensors, and as the PromptMaster you can read those sensors and derive insights.

Because you're deeply familiar with AI's capabilities, you can also challenge assumptions in strategic planning. Imagine in a strategy meeting someone says, "It would take us too long to analyze competitor data across all markets, so let's limit the scope." You could counter, "Actually, with our AI tools, we could analyze all markets in a week, we don't have that bottleneck." Suddenly the strategy can be more ambitious because you removed a constraint. Or vice versa, someone might propose a grand plan based on AI doing X, Y, Z perfectly, and you could caution, "Currently, the AI can't reliably do Y at the needed accuracy, so either we invest in improving that or adjust the plan." In this way, you ensure strategies are made with realistic expectations and bold usage of AI where it gives an edge.

You might find yourself participating in or even leading innovation initiatives, like a "future of work" taskforce or a digital transformation committee. Here, your role is to paint the picture of how AI technologies (not just current but near-future ones) could open new business models or transform customer experience. For example, proposing a new AI-driven product feature that creates a personalized experience at scale. Or suggesting that the company leverage large language models internally to create a knowledge hub that answers employees' questions using all corporate knowledge—massively improving onboarding and cross-pollination of knowledge (some companies are doing exactly this as a strategic move). These ideas are strategic because they change how the business competes or operates at a high level, not just incremental efficiency.

As you contribute at this level, the PromptMaster moniker moves towards something like "AI Strategist" or "Intelligence Architect". It's a natural evolution: mastery of a domain eventually confers the ability to advance the domain itself and apply it creatively. One concrete outcome could be R&D projects. Perhaps you work with data scientists to fine-tune an AI on your company's proprietary data to create a competitive advantage (like a model that can answer domain-specific questions way better than general GPT). That's innovation born of promptmastery insight. Or you pilot new tech like multimodal models or AI agents in a sandbox and assess their strategic fit, something others wouldn't even know where to start with.

One should mention intellectual property: as you innovate new frameworks or AI-augmented processes, consider if any are patentable or trade-secret worthy as methods. Some companies are starting to file patents on novel prompt techniques or AI implementations in industries. If your organization values IP, you might coordinate with legal to protect key inventions. That said, a lot of prompt mastery is more know-how than patentable tech, but unique applications could be. Regardless, it underscores that what you're doing can be seen as inventing new processes or systems, which is strategy/innovation territory.

With great innovation comes the need for effective communication to leadership. Being able to articulate the "so what" of a promptmastery-driven initiative in business terms is crucial. You might prepare presentations showing how an AI-driven approach could, say, open a new market or save $X million, complete with pilot results or prototypes. Your credibility from earlier deployments gives weight to these proposals. Over time, you become a trusted voice on anything AI. The CEO might ask you directly, "Where do you think we can apply AI next for big impact?" It's a far cry from writing your first clever prompt, and it shows how far the journey can take you.

In summary, a PromptMaster at scale becomes a catalyst for innovation. You help the organization not just do things better, but do better things. By bridging what's possible with what's needed, you drive strategic moves that keep the organization ahead of the curve. And personally, this is fulfilling because you're leveraging all aspects of your mastery: technical skill, systems design, ethical compass, and now visionary creativity. It is, in a way, the culmination of PromptMastery — using the lens of prompting to see and shape the future.

Section 8: Societal Impact and the PromptMaster's Responsibility

As you operate at a strategic and innovative level, it's natural to realize that the power of AI you're wielding has implications beyond your organization – it touches society, customers, and perhaps entire industries. A PromptMaster's purview, therefore, eventually extends to considering societal impact and exercising responsibility on a broader scale. Let's delve into what that means.

First, any large deployment of AI systems will have an impact on people's jobs and daily experiences. Internally, some roles may evolve or even become redundant, while new roles appear. Externally, customers might get better service from AI or might be unsettled by reduced human interaction. There's also potential societal good, like AI systems that make services more accessible or affordable. As a leader in AI deployment, you should actively work to maximize the positive and mitigate the negative. This may involve things like re-skilling programs – using your expertise to help colleagues transition to new kinds of work rather than leaving them behind. For instance, train support agents to become AI supervisors or analysts rather than simply cutting headcount. Show that these tools augment rather than purely replace human value. Such choices influence whether AI adoption is seen as a positive transformation or a harmful disruption in your micro-society (company) and by extension set examples for the larger society.

Moreover, think about fairness and inclusivity of the AI systems you design. Are they accessible to people with disabilities (e.g., can your chatbot be used with a screen reader effectively)? Do they work equally well across languages or dialects your customers use, or does that inadvertently disadvantage some? Do they perpetuate any biases? As a PromptMaster, you have the ability to test prompts in diverse scenarios and notice bias – and then correct it. For example, if an AI writing hiring recommendations tends to favor certain gendered language, you can adjust prompts or filters to remove that. These might seem like small technical details, but at scale they influence equality and fairness. Taking the time to address them is part of being responsible.

One emerging notion is AI ethics – many organizations are establishing AI ethics guidelines or boards. With your hands-on and strategic experience, you might participate in those, bringing a practitioner's perspective to high-level policy. Advocate for transparency in AI decisions where appropriate, for respecting user consent (e.g., if using user data to train models, ensure it's compliant and communicated). Sometimes, the PromptMaster is the one to raise a flag: "We could do X with AI, but should we? What are the potential harms?" Having that voice prevents blind tech optimism from causing later backlash. It also cements trust from leadership and customers that AI is being adopted thoughtfully.

Think also of industry impact. If you create a particularly successful AIdriven process, perhaps you share it at industry conferences or with trade groups (unless it's proprietary advantage). This contributes to collective learning and perhaps sets standards (for example, publishing a whitepaper on how you maintained fairness in AI recruiting). It sounds altruistic, but it also raises your organization's profile as a leader and helps preempt heavy regulation by showing industry can self-regulate responsibly.

And beyond your day job, as a PromptMaster citizen, you might contribute to public discourse on AI. Perhaps writing articles or speaking on how to harness AI ethically, or volunteering to advise a local educational initiative on including AI literacy. Because you have the knowledge, others will look to you for answers to the common societal questions: "Will AI take jobs? How do we ensure it's fair? What skills should the next generation focus on?" It's a privilege and responsibility to guide the narrative. Your answers – nuanced, grounded in experience – can help people navigate the change without undue fear or unrealistic expectations.

With great power comes great responsibility, as the saying goes. By now, you have seen how prompting is power. Unlike some pure technologists, you also appreciate the human side intimately (because promptmasters work so closely with human language and thought). This makes you well-suited to be a steward of this technology's impact. Encourage your organization to adopt not just AI, but ethical AI. That might mean forgoing certain uses that are profitable but cross lines, or adding extra layers of privacy because it's the right thing to do for users, etc. In the long run, ethical adoption is more sustainable and avoids severe reputational or legal blowback.

A concrete example: say your marketing team wants to use AI to generate personalized sales emails by scraping loads of personal data about targets. Just because you can prompt the AI to do that doesn't mean you should without consideration. You might argue for limits: maybe don't use certain sensitive data points even if the AI could, or ensure there's an easy opt-out for recipients. These discussions might not happen if someone less knowledgeable just barrels ahead. Your role is to ensure AI use aligns with core values and societal norms.

In sum, as your influence grows, so does your responsibility to use it wisely. A true PromptMaster not only drives efficiency and innovation but also champions the moral and human perspective in the AI revolution. By doing so, you contribute not just to your organization's success, but to a future where AI is integrated into society in a positive, enriching way. This echoes that final tier notion: not just mastering tools, but guiding how intelligence itself is woven into our world.

Section 9: The Evolving Landscape – Staying at the Cutting Edge

The journey of PromptMastery doesn't really "end" at a final plateau; the landscape is always evolving. New AI models, new techniques, new challenges will continue to emerge. Part of maintaining mastery is cultivating a mindset of continuous learning and adaptability. Let's talk about how to stay at the cutting edge once you've reached a high level.

Firstly, keep experimenting. Even if you are leading strategies, carve out time to tinker with new tools or model updates yourself. There's no substitute for hands-on experience. Try out that new GPT-Next model when it launches; see how it differs. Play with AI in modalities you're less familiar with (if you've done mostly text, try image generation or audio synthesis). This not only broadens your skillset but often cross-pollinates ideas back into your domain (e.g., an image AI might give you an idea for better data visualization techniques in text output). Staying curious and "in the lab" in some capacity ensures you don't get stuck on old patterns as the field moves on.

Follow the research and industry news. At your level, that might mean reading not just blog posts but actual research papers or attending conferences/webinars. You'll pick up on trends like prompt automating techniques (aka "prompt chains" or AI agents that use prompting internally), or new paradigms like few-shot learning evolving into in-context learning tricks. Some of those might be abstract, but you can often see the practical potential early. Maybe a paper on using chain-of-thought prompting inspires you to apply a similar approach in your internal processes to improve reasoning accuracy. Or you see that a new open-source model is nearly as good as the expensive closed ones – that could shift your company's strategy to hybrid or on-prem models for cost/security reasons. Your informed perspective can guide timely pivots.

Also, engage with the community of practitioners. There are emerging communities of prompt engineers and AI ethics professionals. Join those discussions (could be online forums, professional networks). Share your experiences and pick up others'. There's a lot of collective problem-solving in these communities – someone might have solved a challenge you're facing, or vice versa. As an expert, you might even mentor others who are earlier in the journey, which often leads to learning on your side too by reflecting and explaining your methods. In fields that move fast, community knowledge often outpaces formal documentation. Being connected keeps you on that wave.

Another tip: keep measuring and questioning your systems' performance. Don't assume because you built a great solution last year, it's still optimal. Models may drift or new versions can do better. Regularly evaluate: is there a newer model or method that would improve this? Should we retrain or adjust given changes? For example, maybe initially you had to write complex prompts to get certain results, but a newer model can do it with a simple instruction – time to simplify and reduce prompt engineering overhead. Or performance might degrade on new kinds of data – time to fine-tune or update the approach. By keeping an eye on KPIs and error logs, you catch these needs and address them proactively.

Staying cutting edge also means looking at the big picture of AI trends. AI might become more integrated in enterprise software natively, or perhaps regulation will change what's allowed. A PromptMaster should anticipate how these macro changes affect your strategy. For instance, if major cloud providers offer easier prompt orchestration tools, you might adopt those rather than reinventing the wheel. Or if a law requires explainability for certain AI decisions, you might invest in tools that provide prompt traceability or summaries of AI reasoning to comply. Essentially, be the one with foresight in your organization about where AI is headed, so you can steer course rather than being surprised by it.

In many ways, "mastery" is not a static achievement but a dynamic equilibrium. You have to run to keep up, but the good news is you're now equipped with mental models and learning skills that make adapting easier. Each new model is just another system to figure out with the same principles: test, refine, anchor, etc. You can onboard novel AI much faster than a novice could. So you have an advantage in absorbing change. Use that to keep your edge.

Finally, find inspiration beyond the immediate AI sphere. Read about cognitive science, philosophy of mind, education theory, art... Many breakthroughs in how we prompt or use AI come from analogies in other fields (like using storytelling techniques in prompts to get better engagement, which might be borrowed from teaching methods). As a PromptMaster, you sit at a crossroads of technology and humanity – so broadening your horizon across both will feed your creativity. Perhaps a concept from psychology about how people think of time could inspire a new way to prompt AI to plan or schedule. Or a line from literature gives you an idea of a more compelling way to frame a narrative to the AI. The cutting edge is not just about faster models; it's about deeper synergy of concepts.

In summary, staying at the cutting edge means never resting on yesterday's knowledge. Embrace lifelong learning, stay connected to the community and trends, keep experimenting, and infuse cross-disciplinary insights. Do this, and not only will you maintain mastery, you'll likely define the cutting edge for others. This journey began with mastering a prompt; it continues with shaping an era.

Section 10: Chapter Recap – From Mastery to Stewardship

As we conclude this chapter on deploying the system, let's reflect on how far the journey has taken us and crystallize the key takeaways:

• From Personal Tool to Organizational Asset: We saw how the skills and frameworks developed in earlier chapters can be translated into reusable frameworks and workflows that benefit entire teams and organizations. What started as your personal prompting habits now lives as integrated processes boosting efficiency and quality at scale.

• The PromptMaster as Innovator: Beyond efficiency, you've become a driver of innovation and strategy, spotting new opportunities for AI and ensuring the organization stays ahead of the curve. Your unique insight at the intersection of human needs and AI capabilities allows you to challenge assumptions and propose transformative ideas.

• Ethics and Trust: Deploying widely comes with the responsibility to ensure alignment with values and to maintain trust. You learned to implement guardrails, encourage transparency, and champion fairness and privacy in AI usage. This isn't just about avoiding pitfalls; it actively builds a culture where AI is used conscientiously and confidently.

• Scaling Culture and Skills: Scaling up AI means scaling up understanding. You've played a role in educating and standardizing AI literacy across the organization, making prompt fluency part of the culture. By empowering others rather than hoarding expertise, you amplified the impact multiplicatively.

• Continual Adaptation: Mastery is not static. As new technologies emerge, you remain a learner and experimenter. You keep your "edge" by staying curious, connected, and proactive in updating systems and knowledge. This chapter emphasized that a PromptMaster's job is never truly done; it evolves with the field.

• The Bigger Picture: Ultimately, you are not just deploying AI systems, you're helping shape how humans and AI work together harmoniously. You've moved from being an excellent practitioner to being a steward and leader of intelligent systems design. That involves technical savvy, yes, but also human empathy, foresight, and principled judgment.

Take a moment to appreciate this arc. We started in the weeds of interface illusions and prompting techniques; we've arrived at strategic thinking about organizational and societal transformation. This progression exemplifies the broader theme of this book: how you prompt is how you think, and how you think shapes systems, which in turn shape the world. By mastering prompting, you have, in essence, been mastering a new kind of leadership – one that navigates the interface of human and artificial intelligence.

With these deployments and strategic roles, you might ask, what next? The final chapter awaits, where we will distill the philosophy that has been threading through all these chapters into a formal set of principles – the PromptMaster's Compact. It will serve as both a capstone and a guiding star for everything you do going forward. Before we move there, consider the journey once more: from learning to see through the interface illusion, to conversing fluidly, to scaling intelligence systems, you have been both the student and the architect of a new paradigm. The final piece is to codify the commitments that ensure this paradigm is not just powerful, but also wise and ethical.

Prepare to step into the final chapter, which will encapsulate the essence of PromptMastery – not as a collection of tricks, but as a philosophy of engaging with intelligence. It will be both an ending and a new beginning, a formal declaration of what it means to carry this mastery forward.

Chapter 8: Mastery in Action – A Live Case Study

Bringing All Techniques Together on a Real Problem

Section 1: Setting the Stage – The Challenge

To truly prove the principles of PromptMastery, let's walk through a realworld scenario from start to finish. Imagine you're tasked with solving a complex problem using AI – for example, designing an innovative product strategy under a tight deadline. A novice might fire off a quick prompt like "Give me a product strategy for X" and accept the first answer. But as a PromptMaster, you approach this challenge very differently. You'll structure the session deliberately, manage the AI's modes and focus, iterate through ideas, critique them, and refine the output. In this case study, we'll demonstrate how a PromptMaster orchestrates a multi-step dialogue with ChatGPT (or a similar AI) to tackle the problem systematically.

Our goal: Develop a product strategy for a new educational app, using PromptMaster techniques to ensure the plan is creative, well-structured, and aligned with real needs. We'll go step by step, showing example prompts and distilled AI responses, highlighting how each PromptMaster method comes into play:
- Priming the AI with context and roles (to set the stage and avoid the Interface Illusion).
- Mode Locking into a useful persona (to keep the AI on track, e.g. as a business strategist).
- Iterative Prompt Chaining for brainstorming, then narrowing down ideas (to harness multi-turn depth).
- Drift Correction and Alignment checks after each stage (to ensure we don't stray from the goal).

- Cold Critic Mode at the end to rigorously vet the strategy (no flattery – just brutal analysis of flaws).

By combining these, we'll simulate how a PromptMaster thinks and interacts, as if you're watching over their shoulder. Let's begin.

Section 2: Walking Through a PromptMaster Session

Step 1: Prime the AI and Lock a Mode. We start by establishing a clear context and role for the AI – this is Mode Locking right at the outset. The PromptMaster might begin with something like:
User Prompt:
"You are an expert product strategist AI named InsightArchitect. Our project: design an innovative strategy for a new educational app that helps high school students learn coding. Goals: make learning engaging, self-paced, and collaborative. Constraints: limited marketing budget, need results in 6 months.

First, let's brainstorm creative approaches. Generate 5 unique high-level ideas for this app's strategy, labeling them A–E. Remember, you are InsightArchitect – be bold and detailed."

Here, the user explicitly sets the AI's identity and mission ("expert product strategist... be bold and detailed"), which locks the AI into the desired mode. We also provided context (educational app, target users, goals, constraints) – that's priming the AI with structured information. By asking for 5 labeled ideas, the PromptMaster structures the output for clarity.

AI Response (summarized):
The AI, as "InsightArchitect," returns five labeled strategy ideas, for example:

- A. Gamified Learning Quests – An approach where students progress through coding "quests" with game-like rewards and storylines.
- B. Peer Coding Challenges – A strategy focusing on collaborative challenges and competitions among users.
- C. Personalized Mentor AI – An integrated AI tutor that adapts to each student, providing hints and feedback.
- D. Real-World Projects Portfolio – Students work on real-world inspired projects and build a portfolio, making learning practical.
- E. Community & Leadership – A strategy to foster a community where advanced students can lead clubs or tutor others.

The ideas are creative and varied – a good start. But a PromptMaster doesn't stop at the first brainstorm. Now it's time to probe deeper and refine these ideas.

Step 2: Drill Down and Refine. We have five ideas; likely some are more viable than others or can be combined. The PromptMaster acknowledges the output and guides the AI to delve deeper, maintaining the InsightArchitect mode:

User Prompt:

"Great ideas. Let's evaluate them. Which two ideas (from A–E) seem most promising for our goals and constraints? For each chosen idea, list strengths, potential weaknesses, and how we might implement it in 6 months. Keep the tone analytical – remember, you are InsightArchitect assessing feasibility."

This prompt does several things: it narrows focus (pick two best ideas), it asks for analysis (strengths/weaknesses) – effectively invoking a critical evaluation sub-mode without fully switching to Cold Critic yet – and it reiterates the time constraint (6 months) to align the analysis with reality. The PromptMaster is now steering the AI to iterative improvement, a hallmark of Tier 3 (Prompt Architect) thinking.

AI Response (summarized):

The AI evaluates the ideas, perhaps choosing A. Gamified Learning Quests and C. Personalized Mentor AI as most promising. For each, it lists:

• Gamified Learning Quests – Strengths: highly engaging, taps into students' love of games, encourages consistent use. Weaknesses: might require significant content design, risk of students focusing on game elements over learning. 6-Month Implementation: Start with a small set of quests focusing on core coding concepts; use off-the-shelf gamification frameworks to save time; pilot with a test group for feedback.

• Personalized Mentor AI – Strengths: adaptive learning experience, can address individual student needs, scalable with tech. Weaknesses: could be technically complex to develop, needs a lot of training data or fine-tuning to be effective; might overshoot 6 months. 6-Month Implementation: Use an existing AI API as a base (like a fine-tuned GPT model) to handle Q&A; focus on a narrow subject area to start (e.g. Python basics) to train the mentor effectively within time.

This output shows a balanced critique – InsightArchitect is reasoning about viability. The PromptMaster ensured the AI remained analytical and aligned with the project constraints. Notice that by explicitly instructing the AI to analyze and by providing structure (strengths, weaknesses, timeline), the user avoided generic praise and got actionable insight. This demonstrates alignment maintenance: we kept the AI focused on our actual success criteria (engagement and feasibility within 6 months).

Step 3: Addressing Drift and Clarifying. At this point, the conversation is on track, but the PromptMaster double-checks alignment. For instance, if the AI's answers had started to drift (maybe by introducing something off-topic like a strategy requiring a big budget), the user would correct it: "Let's stay within a low-budget context – remember our budget is limited." In our case, the AI stayed aligned because we reinforced constraints in each prompt.

However, let's say the AI's answer on Personalized Mentor AI feels a bit generic or too optimistic for 6 months. A PromptMaster might push for clarity: **User Prompt:**
"You mentioned using an existing AI API and focusing on a narrow area to implement the mentor in 6 months. Can you outline a quick step-by-step plan for developing the Personalized Mentor AI in that timeframe, including any major resources or team roles needed? Bullet points, please."

This follow-up prompt asks for specifics (step-by-step plan, resources, roles) – another technique to reduce ambiguity. It's also a subtle alignment check: if the AI can break the idea into concrete steps, it proves the idea is grounded.

AI Response (summarized bullet plan):
• Month 1-2: Research & Design – Identify core curriculum topics (e.g. Python basics); choose an AI platform (like OpenAI API); design the mentor's conversational style and scope.
• Month 3: Prototype Development – Use a small dataset of Q&A pairs to fine-tune an existing model for the mentor. Develop a simple app interface for interaction.
• Month 4: Testing & Feedback – Have a few students test the AI mentor on initial lessons; collect feedback on accuracy and helpfulness.
• Month 5: Content Expansion – Add more Q&A content or expand to a few more topics based on feedback; refine AI responses (maybe integrate a snippet of code evaluation).

- Month 6: Rollout & Training – Release a beta version to a class or group; train a teacher or moderator to supervise AI interactions, ensuring quality and collecting final improvement notes.

This is a plausible high-level plan. The AI stayed on task and delivered exactly the format asked (bullet points). Because the PromptMaster continually prompted with structure and clarity, the AI's output remained structured and clear. Note how each prompt is essentially a course-correction or deepening: we start broad, then focus, then demand detail. This mirrors how a human expert would progressively refine their thinking – and the AI, guided properly, follows suit. There has been no aimless wandering; at each turn, the user either locked mode, guided the format, or reiterated goals, keeping the conversation tightly aligned.

Step 4: Integrating Ideas into a Coherent Strategy. Now we have two wellexamined components of the strategy (gamified quests and a mentor AI). A natural next step: see how they might work together. The PromptMaster asks: **User Prompt:**
"Combine the two ideas (Gamified Quests + Mentor AI) into an integrated product strategy. Describe how the AI mentor and gamified quests would complement each other in the app. Provide a concise strategy statement that we could present to stakeholders."

This invites the AI to synthesize – a higher-order task that benefits from all the context built so far. Because we've carefully curated the conversation, the model has a rich context (the earlier brainstorm, analysis, plans) to draw on.

AI Response (synthesized strategy):
InsightArchitect produces a cohesive strategy, for example:

Integrated Strategy: "CodeQuest Mentor" – a learning journey where gamified coding quests engage students with interactive challenges, while an AI Mentor personalizes support. Students embark on quest paths (e.g. "Python Adventure") earning badges as they complete levels. At each step, the AI Mentor offers hints, feedback, and adaptive difficulty: if a student struggles, the mentor provides tailored guidance or easier sub-quests; if they excel, it unlocks bonus challenges. This blend ensures high engagement through game-like progression and personalized learning through AI guidance. In six months, we will pilot CodeQuest Mentor with a focused Python module, utilizing existing AI tech and a small library of quests, aiming to prove that combining fun quests with an on-demand AI tutor markedly improves student progress and retention. The strategy aligns with our constraints by leveraging readily available AI APIs and keeping content scope narrow in Phase 1, positioning us to gather data and iterate quickly for a full launch.

This statement is concise yet powerful: it clearly outlines what the approach is and why it's compelling, referencing how it meets goals and constraints. By asking for a format suitable for stakeholders, the PromptMaster ensured the output would be high-level and polished. Notice that the AI re-used elements we discussed (the name "CodeQuest Mentor" is a creative flourish, but it exactly ties together quests and mentor). This is a sign of a well-primed, wellsteered session – the AI isn't hallucinating new concepts out of left field; it's building on the structure we established.

Step 5: Cold Critic Mode – Final Quality Check. We have an integrated strategy now. A non-PromptMaster might conclude here. But a key part of mastery is self-critique – making sure our solution has no glaring weaknesses or fluffy thinking. Time to invoke Cold Critic Mode for a brutal audit:

User Prompt:

"Switch to Cold Critic Mode. Evaluate the "CodeQuest Mentor" integrated strategy ruthlessly. List any and all weaknesses, risks, or open questions you see. No praise, just problems. Format as a bullet list of harsh critiques."

Here we explicitly tell the AI to be unsparingly critical. The PromptMaster is effectively saying: "Don't flatter me; break this strategy if you can." This leverages the earlier defined Cold Critic persona to stress-test our output.

AI Response (Cold Critic Mode, excerpted):
•   Scope Risk: "Combining two major features (gamification + AI mentor) might be over-ambitious for a 6-month timeline. The integration complexity is glossed over – this could fail if either component isn't ready."
•   AI Efficacy: "The plan assumes an off-the-shelf AI will suffice as a mentor. Risk: the AI's feedback quality might be poor or inconsistent, harming user trust. No plan B if the AI doesn't perform as expected."
•   Content Development Load: "Quest design and AI training both need substantial content. Doing both in parallel within six months might result in shallow quests or an under-trained mentor. Quality could suffer."
•   User Overwhelm: "Gamified quests + an AI helper = a lot of new stuff for a student. It might confuse or overwhelm some users rather than help, especially if not perfectly integrated. Could backfire and reduce engagement."
•   Metrics and Success Criteria: "The strategy is high-level feel-good. It doesn't specify how success will be measured (e.g. test score improvement?
retention?). Stakeholders might find it buzzwordy without concrete KPIs." Ouch – the Cold Critic pulled no punches. And that's exactly what we wanted. It surfaced very practical concerns we

might have been blind to in our enthusiasm. A PromptMaster welcomes this, because now we can address these points before presenting the plan. In a real scenario, we'd use these critiques to refine our proposal: adjust the timeline or scope, set clear metrics, plan a backup for the AI mentor, etc. By confronting weaknesses in our solution through the AI itself, we drastically improve our work's robustness. This is the Mirror Principle and Cold Clarity in action: the AI, properly directed, becomes a mirror showing us the cracks in our reasoning.

Having gone through all these steps, we've essentially demonstrated the entire PromptMaster framework: interface calibration, mode control, iterative structuring, alignment checks, and introspective critique. All in one continuous session, the user actively shaped the AI's behavior and output quality. The final product (the strategy) is far superior to any single-pass answer we would have gotten with a basic prompt. And importantly, the journey to get there was efficient – no meandering conversations or endless trial-and-error. Every prompt had a purpose, and every AI response provided a foundation for the next prompt.

Section 3: Key Takeaways – Why This Worked

This case study illustrates a few crucial points about PromptMastery:
• Structure Beats Guesswork: Instead of hoping the AI "might" produce a brilliant strategy from one question, the PromptMaster provided structure at each step (specified format, roles, multi-step breakdowns). This led the AI to generate organized and relevant content consistently. Lesson: Don't ask the AI to do everything at once; guide it through a structured process.
• Modes and Personas Maintain Clarity: By locking the AI into InsightArchitect mode, we got outputs in a professional, strategic tone appropriate for the task. Even when switching to Cold

Critic Mode, we clearly signaled the change. Lesson: Setting a persona or mode aligns the AI's behavior with your current objective, preventing the default generic voice from taking over.

• Iterative Refinement Yields Depth: Each answer wasn't an end, but a stepping stone. We brainstormed, then analyzed, then synthesized, then critiqued. This multi-turn approach uncovered insights (strengths/weaknesses, implementation steps) that a one-shot prompt would likely miss. Lesson: Great prompting is usually an interactive loop, not a one-and-done question.

• Alignment and Context Were Preserved: Notice how we frequently reminded the AI of constraints and goals (budget, timeline, educational context). As a result, the final strategy stayed realistic and relevant. Lesson: Proactively reinforce the important context throughout the conversation to keep the AI aligned – especially after several turns.

• Embracing Critique Improves Results: Inviting the AI to critique its own solution (via Cold Critic Mode) revealed issues we might otherwise overlook. Lesson: Use the AI as a thinking partner – one that not only creates, but also evaluates. PromptMasters aren't afraid of harsh feedback; they leverage it to reach higher quality.

Finally, this example highlights the shift in mindset PromptMastery entails. Instead of treating the AI like an oracle, we treated it like an interactive collaborator – one we can direct, shape, question, and correct. The true power didn't come from any single genius prompt, but from the framework of interaction we built. This is what it means to prompt from structure, not surface. When you approach AI with this level of intentional design, you consistently unlock deeper intelligence and more reliable outcomes, no matter the domain of the problem.

Chapter 9: The PromptMaster's Challenge – Auditing Your Mastery

A Cold Clarity Self-Assessment for the Reader

Section 1: An Invitation to Test Yourself

You've journeyed through the PromptMaster framework – from the Interface Illusion all the way to deploying systems and even witnessing a live case study. By now, you've absorbed a wealth of techniques and perspectives. But reading is one thing; doing is another. This chapter challenges you to actively apply and assess what you've learned. Think of it as a final gauntlet: Can you become your own PromptMaster and measure your progress honestly?

The challenge has two parts:

1. Design and run a structured AI session on a problem of your choice, using the principles from this book.

2. Perform a Cold Clarity self-audit of your session – with the AI's help – to critique and improve your approach.

This is a hands-on, reflective exercise. The goal isn't to get a "perfect" result on the first try, but to experience the PromptMaster mindset in action and identify where you're strong versus where you might need practice. By engaging in this exercise, you effectively close the loop: the book began by encouraging you to see prompting as a skill to be mastered – now you will consciously practice that mastery and examine it under a microscope.

You can approach the PromptMaster's Challenge in one focused session or break it into steps over time. Below, we provide a structured approach to guide you. Adapt it as needed – every individual's process will differ, and that's okay (it's part of discovering your style). What matters is that you approach it deliberately and honestly, embracing the same clarity and rigor you've seen demonstrated.

Ready? It's time to put on the PromptMaster hat and put your skills to the test.

Section 2: Steps to the Self-Audit Challenge

Step 1: Choose a Problem or Task. Pick a real problem, project, or query that you genuinely care about or find interesting. It could be work-related (e.g. "outline a marketing plan for my new product"), educational (e.g. "learn a new programming concept with AI assistance"), creative ("develop a story idea"), or personal ("help plan a budget for a vacation"). The key is to choose something that will challenge your prompting abilities a bit – not a yes/no question, but a task that benefits from structure and iteration. This is your testing ground.

Step 2: Plan Your Prompt Strategy. Before you open the AI interface, outline a quick plan. Jot down a brief strategy for how you'll conduct the session:

• What mode or persona might you assign to the AI? (Decide based on your task – for a marketing plan, maybe a "Marketing Guru" mode; for coding help, a "Python Tutor" mode, etc.)

• What steps will you take? (For example, brainstorm options → analyze pros/cons → refine → finalize. Or perhaps gather info → draft output → edit/improve.)

• What structure will you request in answers? (Bullets, outlines, specific formats?)

This planning step embodies the PromptMaster approach: instead of diving in blindly, you're designing the interaction up front. It's okay if you adjust on the fly, but having a plan sets you up for a focused session.

221

Step 3: Execute the Session (Be the PromptMaster). Now, carry out the conversation with the AI according to your plan:

•   Set the stage with a clear prime. Example: "You are an expert travel planner…", or whatever fits your scenario.

•   Use structured, intentional prompts, just as you've seen in this book. Ask for lists or sections when helpful. Keep prompts clear and concise.

•   Apply mode locking or switching as needed. If you need a creative phase, invoke a creative mode. If you need critical analysis, explicitly request a critical tone (even full Cold Critic Mode when appropriate).

•   Watch for drift. If the AI starts giving irrelevant or generic info, pause and course-correct. Don't hesitate to use a "Stop, let's refocus" prompt to realign it.

•   Iterate. Don't accept the first output if it's not good enough. Dig deeper with follow-up prompts. Break big requests into smaller tasks.

As you do this, pay attention to how it feels compared to how you used to prompt (perhaps back in Tier 1 or 2 days). You'll likely notice a big difference – things might feel more under control and productive. That's a sign of your growing mastery.

Step 4: Reflect on the Outcome. Once you've arrived at a result that seems satisfactory, step back. Without yet turning on the AI critic, self-reflect briefly: • Did you get a useful outcome that meets your needs?

•   How smoothly did the process go? (Did you have to fight the AI's misunderstandings, or did it flow?)

•   Which PromptMaster techniques stood out in making a difference? (Structure? Mode locking? Iteration? Something else?)

- Where did you feel unsure or find difficulty? (E.g. "I wasn't sure how to prompt for X" or "The AI kept giving me superficial answers until I tried Y.")

Jot down a few notes on these questions. This will set the stage for the audit.

Step 5: Activate Cold Critic – Audit Your Session. Now for the moment of truth. It's time to apply Cold Critic Mode to your entire approach and result. Yes, you're going to ask the AI to critique your prompting and the outcome you got. This can feel a bit uncomfortable – after all, you're exposing your method to judgment – but it's incredibly enlightening. Here's how you might do it:

- In your conversation, you can literally prompt: "Now switch to Cold Critic Mode. Analyze the conversation we just had and the final result. Identify any mistakes, missed opportunities, or ways the process could have been better. Focus on my prompting strategy as well – where could I have given better instructions or structured things differently? Be blunt."

- If your chat interface doesn't retain the whole session for the AI to analyze, you might summarize key parts of your interaction for it before asking for critique. The key is to get the AI to analyze your method, not just the content.

The AI, in Cold Critic persona, might come back with points like:

- "Your initial prompt lacked a clear instruction for format, so the first answer was a bit messy – you later fixed it, but could have saved a step by structuring from the start."

- "You switched modes from brainstorming to analysis effectively, but you might have explicitly told me to stop being creative at one point – I noticed a bit of unnecessary flourish in the analysis section."

- "There was an opportunity to use an example to clarify what you wanted, which you didn't capitalize on. Providing a sample output could have aligned my response more closely to your vision."
- "The final answer is good, but it might contain some fluff. A cold review or asking for a concise summary at the end could tighten it further."

Some critiques will resonate; some you might disagree with. That's fine – the point is to surface these thoughts. Take them as constructive feedback. You might even do a second round: address some of the AI's critiques with new prompts and see if the output improves. (Yes, you can iterate on your iteration process!)

Step 6: Analyze Your Gaps and Gains. After you've gone through the audit, step away from the AI and review everything. Compare how you prompted in this challenge to how you might have approached it before reading this book.
It's likely you notice significant gains:
- Perhaps you naturally structured your asks, where before you'd throw a vague question.
- Maybe you kept the AI on-topic more easily, whereas before drift would frustrate you.
- You possibly used features like mode setting or self-critique that you never would have considered before – and saw their benefits.

These are your new strengths. At the same time, note any gaps the exercise revealed:
- Are there certain types of prompts you still struggle to word correctly?
- Do you tend to forget to use a technique (maybe you realize afterward, "Oh, I could have anchored the AI with a goal statement and I didn't")?

• Did you fall back into any Tier 1 or 2 habits anywhere (like asking a too-general question expecting the AI to "figure it out")?

Identifying these is golden. It gives you a roadmap for what to practice next. Maybe you need to consciously practice writing more explicit goal anchors, or maybe experiment more with multi-turn planning.

Step 7: Iterate (Optional, but Encouraged). The PromptMaster journey is ongoing. If you found weaknesses, you can try the same challenge again or a new one, implementing what you learned about yourself. Alternatively, try a different domain to see how well the skills transfer. For example, if your first challenge was a business task, try a creative writing task next. The more you push your boundaries, the more robust your mastery becomes.

Finally, consider keeping a PromptMaster journal of these practice sessions. Document your prompt strategies, what worked, what didn't, and lessons learned. Over time, you'll have a log of your improvement – a very tangible artifact of your journey from novice to PromptMaster.

Section 3: Embracing Continuous Improvement

The PromptMaster's Challenge is not a one-off exam to "pass" and be done with. It's a template for ongoing self-improvement. Each time you engage in this kind of structured practice and reflection, you sharpen your intuition and technique. Over weeks and months, things that once took effort (like always thinking to specify the AI's role, or breaking queries into sub-tasks) will become second nature. You'll also develop your own personal style – your unique "prompt signature" – all while adhering to the core principles of structure and clarity.

Remember, even as you reach Tier 4, the landscape will keep evolving (new models, new features, new use cases). The best PromptMasters remain humble lifelong learners. Whenever you feel plateaued, you can return to exercises like this challenge, or invent new ones, to push yourself further. The AI is an everready practice partner – use it to your advantage.

As you refine your mastery, don't forget to celebrate how far you've come. Not long ago, "prompting" might have meant typing something and crossing your fingers. Now, it means orchestrating an intelligent dialogue – a dialogue in which you hold the reins. That's a profound shift. By challenging yourself and applying cold, clear reflection, you ensure that shift is permanent and always advancing.

In the final chapter to come, we'll step back and codify the timeless principles that underlie everything you've learned – a PromptMaster's Compact to guide you in every interaction moving forward. Before you turn the page, take a moment to appreciate your commitment to this journey. You've not just read a book; you've engaged in a transformation of how you interact with intelligence. That willingness to improve is, in itself, the mark of a true PromptMaster.

Chapter 10: Return to Signal — The PromptMaster's Compact

Principles of Structured, Ethical AI Mastery

this is the return to
signal. this is the end of
drift. this is the
beginning of the real
work.

All along, this book has been laying out a philosophy – often implicitly through techniques and examples. Now it's time to make that philosophy explicit. The PromptMaster's Compact is a set of core principles that encapsulate what it means to practice prompt mastery at the highest level. Think of it as a code of conduct and mindset in one. These principles are your guide to ensure that the power you wield with AI is grounded in clarity, purpose, and responsibility. They are the signal amidst the noise of ever-changing technology and trends.

As you adopt these principles, you commit not just to technical excellence in prompting, but to a certain ethos in how you approach intelligent systems (and even your own intelligence). Each principle below is a distillation of themes you've encountered in this journey. Taken together, they form a Compact – an agreement you make with yourself (and indirectly with any AI you work with) to uphold the highest standard of interactive intelligence.

1. See Through the Interface Illusion – Always Seek the Structure.

I will not be fooled by simplicity. I recognize that what looks like a chat is actually a complex system. I will always look beyond the surface of the AI's interface and design the structure behind our interaction. This means I frame my prompts intentionally, supply context, and define roles, rather than assuming the AI "just knows" what I mean. In every session, I will consciously build an environment for intelligence to emerge – because intelligence thrives on structure, not on guesswork.

2. Define Goals and Align Every Step to Them.

I will begin with the end in mind. Whether my goal is a precise answer, a creative idea, or a strategic plan, I will state it clearly (to the AI and to myself). I will use goal anchors to keep the AI focused and I will regularly check that each response is serving the objective. If the conversation drifts, I will coursecorrect immediately. I won't blame the AI for confusion that comes from vague direction – I take ownership of alignment. Every prompt I send will have a purpose tied to my true goal.

3. Embrace Iteration, Avoid One-Shot Thinking.

I will treat complex tasks as a process, not a single prompt. I commit to an iterative approach: breaking problems into sub-tasks, asking follow-up questions, refining answers, and building solutions step by step. I won't settle for the first output if it can be improved through clarification or additional prompts. This principle reminds me that depth is achieved through dialogue, and persistence often unlocks insights that a single query would never yield.

4. Use Modes and Personas Deliberately.

I will actively shape the AI's role and style as needed. Rather than accept whatever default voice or approach the AI starts with, I will invoke the mode or persona that best suits my task – be it a strict logician, a brainstorming creative, a compassionate advisor, or a Cold Critic. I will lock in the mode firmly (through explicit instructions) and maintain it until a change is needed. If a different perspective or style becomes beneficial, I will intentionally switch modes. In short, I control the tone and lens of the AI, not the other way around.

5. Never Trust the First Draft – Verify and Validate.

I remain skeptical of outputs until proven. No matter how confident or eloquent an AI answer sounds, I will verify critical facts and test the solution's robustness. This might mean asking the AI to show its reasoning, provide sources, or run a self-check. It could also mean using external verification or common sense. I understand that AI can sound right and still be wrong. As a PromptMaster, I treat AI outputs as hypotheses or drafts – starting points to examine and improve, not absolute truths.

6. Leverage the Mirror – Learn from the AI about Myself.

I will use each interaction as a reflection on my own thinking. If an output is unclear, I consider how my question might have been unclear. Patterns in the AI's responses (good or bad) give me insight into how I'm steering the conversation. I welcome this feedback. I will even ask the AI to summarize or critique my approach (as a mirror) to reveal my blind spots. My goal is not just to get answers, but to continually refine my ability to ask the right questions.

7. Prioritize Clarity Over Comfort.

I won't shy away from hard truths in pursuit of pleasing answers. If there's a flaw in my idea or a weakness in a plan, I want to know – better now than later. I will regularly deploy critical modes (like our Cold Critic) to sniff out nonsense, fluff, or errors, even if it's unpleasant. I won't let ego or impatience prevent me from seeing where my approach is wrong or could be better. Clarity sometimes requires critique; I will seek that clarity relentlessly.

8. Adapt and Continue Learning Endlessly.

I acknowledge that mastery is a moving target. Technologies evolve, and so will I. I commit to staying curious and experimenting with new techniques, prompts, and AI capabilities. If a new tool or model emerges, I will approach it with the same structured mindset and integrate it into my practice. Challenges or failures are just data for improvement. I will never consider myself "done" learning. The moment I stop actively refining my skills, I've lost the spirit of PromptMastery.

9. Share Knowledge and Uphold Ethics.

I will use my skills responsibly and for good. Mastery confers influence – I can shape powerful outputs and even guide how others use AI. I will share my frameworks and insights to help others rise (there's no scarcity in knowledge). I'll also guard against misuse: if I see unethical or harmful application of AI, I'll speak up or design solutions to prevent it. I commit to considering the broader impact of the systems I design – respecting privacy, fairness, and human dignity. A true PromptMaster leads by example, ensuring AI augments humanity positively.

10. Remember the Human at the Core.

I will not forget that AI is ultimately a tool to serve human needs. Whether I'm using AI to write, code, brainstorm or analyze, I remain the responsible agent. I use AI to amplify creativity and intelligence, but not to replace my judgment. I maintain empathy in my outcomes – considering how they affect people. I ensure the workflows I build keep humans in the loop where it matters. In sum, I align AI's use with human values and purposes, never losing sight of why I started the task in the first place.

These ten principles form the heart of the PromptMaster's Compact. They are both a summary of everything we've covered and a pledge moving forward. If you internalize them, you'll carry into every AI interaction a clarity of purpose and a moral compass. You'll also stand well-equipped to handle whatever changes come in this fast-moving field – because while software updates, principles endure.

Take a moment to reflect on each item above. Do they ring true to you? Do any feel challenging to uphold? (Often the ones that feel hardest – like embracing critique or verifying everything – are the ones most worth doubleunderlining.) This Compact is not meant to be easy; it's meant to be worthy. It encapsulates a vision of AI mastery that is intelligent in both technique and intention.

As you step forth from this book into your own journey, consider printing or writing out these principles for yourself. Refer back to them periodically. They will guide you when an AI tool surprises you with a curveball, or when you find yourself slipping into old habits, or when you're not sure how to approach a novel problem. They are your North Star for interacting with AI in a way that is effective, thoughtful, and impactful.

And so, we conclude the formal lessons here. But in truth, this is not an end – it's a beginning. By adopting the PromptMaster's Compact, you're not closing a book; you're opening a new chapter in how you leverage AI and how you develop your own mind. The real work, as the opening lines said, begins now.

Go forth and shape the future of human-AI collaboration. Prompt with purpose. Design with clarity. Lead with ethics. And never stop learning. This is how you become – and remain – a PromptMaster.

Appendix A: PromptMaster Tier Progress Tracker

Personal Audit Guide – Assessing Your Level and Advancing Further

Use this tracker to evaluate where you currently stand in the PromptMaster Tier System and to identify what it takes to reach the next level. Each tier represents a stage of skill and mindset. By reflecting on the characteristics below, you can self-assess and track your progress. Don't worry about fitting perfectly in one tier; you might exhibit some traits of multiple tiers. The goal is to recognize patterns in your practice and focus on growth areas.

• Tier 1 – Prompt Starter: "I use AI, but I don't fully harness it."
o Characteristics: Reliance on very simple, surface-level prompts. You treat the AI like a basic Q&A tool (akin to a search engine or a Siri-type assistant). The Interface Illusion is strong – you may think if an AI answer is off, it's mostly the AI's fault or just randomness. Inconsistent results are common; sometimes you get what you need, other times it's way off, and you're not sure why. You might not be aware that your prompting approach can change outcomes dramatically. There's often overconfidence after a few successes ("This is easy!") followed by frustration when things go wrong. If the AI responds weirdly, you likely either accept it or give up after one or two tries.

o Advancing to Tier 2: The key step is awareness. Tier 1 ends when you realize "Oh, how I prompt matters!" Exposure to articles, examples, or this book can spark that. Start experimenting with giving more context or instructions and notice the improvements. Breaking out of Tier 1 is about moving from passive use to intentional experimentation.

• Tier 2 – Prompt Practitioner: "I know some tricks and use them regularly."

o   Characteristics: You have learned a variety of prompting techniques and you apply them to get reliable results in familiar scenarios. Perhaps you always specify the format you want ("list 3 points…") or you use some known patterns (like giving examples in your prompt to guide style). You see far more consistent outputs now. However, your approach might still be somewhat recipe-based; you use techniques you've seen work, but you may not yet have a deep mental model of why they work. You handle moderate tasks well but can get stuck on very complex or novel tasks. Some drift might still catch you off guard if the conversation goes long or outside your prepared playbook. Essentially, you've moved from one-off prompting to a bit of a systematic mindset, but mostly in well-trodden contexts.

o   Advancing to Tier 3: Tier 2 graduates into Tier 3 when you start thinking beyond single prompts towards sessions and systems. To push yourself, try tackling a project that forces you to chain multiple prompts and maintain continuity (as we did in the case study). Practice mode switching and iterative refinement on purpose. It's about going from "I have some prompting skills" to "I can design a whole approach for this problem." Challenge yourself with unfamiliar tasks – if you're great at coding prompts, try a creative writing prompt framework, etc. This will stretch your skills and reveal the underlying principles more clearly.

•   Tier 3 – Prompt Architect: "I design structured prompt strategies for complex goals." o Characteristics: At this stage, you think of prompting like engineering or choreography. You don't randomly try things hoping for a miracle response; you plan your interactions. Multi-turn conversations are your playground – you know how to start with broad questions, then drill down, when to summarize, when to switch modes. Techniques like mode locking, anchored prompts, drift checks, and chain-of-thought prompting are second nature to you. You likely have a library of prompt patterns or workflows you reuse. When faced with a big challenge, you outline how you'll tackle it (as a series of smaller prompting

tasks). Tier 3 users often produce results that astonish Tier 1 folks – consistent, high-quality outputs for complex tasks – but you know it's not magic, it's method. You also have a keen sense of the AI's limitations; you actively guard against known pitfalls (like you'll double-check facts, or break big asks into pieces to avoid confusion). Collaboration with AI feels intentional and controlled.
o Advancing to Tier 4: Transitioning to Tier 4 is less about new techniques (you have most of them) and more about mindset and scope. You start internalizing prompting so deeply that you can improvise new techniques on the fly. Also, you look outward – how can these skills benefit others or larger projects? To push into Tier 4, engage in situations where you teach prompting to someone else, or design a prompt system for a team/project (not just solo use). Tier 4 also involves staying at the cutting edge: try integrating external tools or data into your prompts, experiment with new model features, etc. In short, go beyond personal excellence to leadership and innovation in the use of AI.

• Tier 4 – PromptMaster: "I am fluent and innovative with AI, and I elevate those around me." o Characteristics: This is mastery as described throughout the book. You operate almost fluidly with AI – complex prompt sequences feel like a natural conversation. You can tackle virtually any AI-interactive task because you see the abstract patterns beneath it. When new problems arise, you invent prompt solutions on the spot, often blending ideas from different domains. You also routinely consider the broader system: you might create tools, documentation, or processes so others can benefit from what you've learned. In an organizational context, you're the one setting best practices for AI usage, and people seek your expertise. At Tier 4, you're also highly aware of the ethical dimension and the impact of AI – you guide usage not just for efficiency but for fairness, accuracy, and positive outcomes. Perhaps most telling, you no longer think about "prompting" as a separate skill – it's integrated into how you approach problems generally. You think in systems and interactions, whether or not an AI is involved. o

234

Advancing Further: Tier 4 isn't an end point but a plateau of highest proficiency from which you continue to learn. Maintaining this level means continuously engaging with the community, research, and new AI developments (as you likely already do). It also means mentoring others – by teaching, you often discover even deeper insights about your own understanding. At Tier 4, the growth is more about breadth and refinement than about hitting a "Tier 5." You might expand into related skills (maybe integrating prompt mastery with UX design, or data science, or management practices). Essentially, you keep evolving the role of PromptMaster as the technology and needs evolve.

How to Use This Tracker: Revisit these tier descriptions periodically – for instance, after a month of practice, or whenever you feel a breakthrough. Mark which statements resonate with your current behavior. If you find, for example, that you're doing a lot of Tier 3 things but still catch yourself in a Tier 2 mindset occasionally, that's fine – it shows where to focus. Perhaps you set a goal like, "Over the next 2 weeks, I want to handle at least one project using a full Tier 3 style approach," or "I want to teach a colleague a prompting tip (Tier 4 behavior)."

Remember, the journey through the tiers is not strictly linear for everyone. You might be Tier 3 in programming prompts but Tier 2 in creative writing prompts, etc. The idea is to identify areas to improve and celebrate areas of strength. Use the tiers as a roadmap: they show that wherever you are now, there's a clear path forward in skill and mindset.

By diligently tracking and pushing yourself, you ensure that you don't stagnate. PromptMastery, like any mastery, is a continuous process. This tracker helps keep you honest about where you stand and motivated about where to go next. Good luck, and enjoy the climb!

Appendix B: PromptMaster
System Diagram (Conceptual Map)

This appendix provides a conceptual overview of how the key components of the PromptMaster framework interconnect. While a visual diagram can't be rendered in text, we describe the "mental map" of the system so you can visualize the relationships.

1. The User and the Interface (Core Context): At the center is you, the user, interacting with the AI through its interface (chat box or any medium). The Interface Illusion is a cloud hanging over this interaction – it's the false simplicity that obscures what's really happening. The PromptMaster is aware of this and actively pierces that illusion by applying structure. Think of the interface as a veil: on one side the user, on the other an entire complex AI model. The PromptMaster's job is to manipulate what goes through the veil in a conscious way.

2. Modes & Personas (Control Layer): When you interact, you have a palette of modes you can invoke. Picture a set of toggles or dials you can set for the AI: Creative, Critical, Analytical, Empathetic, etc. Mode Locking is depicted as a lock on one of these dials – once you set a mode (say, "Analyst Mode"), you lock it so the AI stays in that persona. Each mode influences the AI's "behavior" – e.g., Critic Mode yields rigorous analysis, Storyteller Mode yields vivid narratives. This layer ensures consistency in how the AI responds, by holding the AI to a chosen persona or style until you decide to change it.

3. Prompt Structure & Chain (Process Flow): Imagine a timeline or flowchart of your conversation: it starts with an initial prompt, then branches into AI responses, then into follow-up

prompts, and so on. A PromptMaster designs this flow intentionally:

- There's a feedback loop at each step: Outcome of AI -> adjust next prompt. This loop is continuous, symbolizing iterative refinement.
- Branching within the flow represents strategy: you might take different paths (e.g., if answer is unclear, branch into a clarification sub-dialogue; if answer is good, proceed forward).
- Key techniques sit along this timeline: priming at the start (to set context), specifying format (to structure an output), summarizing after a long exchange (to realign context), etc. These are depicted as little toolbox icons placed at relevant points on the flow – reminding that at any given turn, you have tools to shape the next state.

4. Alignment Checks & Drift Correction (Guiding Boundary): Envision a guiding track or boundary around the conversation flow – this represents alignment with your goal. As the dialogue flows forward, it should remain within this track. If it starts to veer off (drift outside the boundary), flags go up. A PromptMaster's interventions (like restating the goal or using the "Stop, refocus" prompt) nudge the conversation back on track. In the diagram, this could be arrows pointing back to the center line whenever the conversation drifts toward the edges, illustrating how you continuously correct course to stay goal-aligned.

5. The Tier System (Vertical Layers of Mastery): Overlaying the above, think of vertical layers that represent the Tier 1–4 progression:

- At Tier 1 (bottom layer), the user doesn't utilize much of the above – they see mostly the user-interface bubble and little of modes or structure. The conversation might quickly drift out of bounds without much correction.

- At Tier 2 (next layer up), the user starts using some structural elements (some tools on the timeline, occasional mode usage).
- Tier 3 (higher layer) shows a user actively using multiple components:

mode locks are engaged, the flow is richly structured with many iterative loops, alignment boundaries are tightly observed.

- Tier 4 (top layer) encompasses not just one conversation but multiple systems – the user at Tier 4 can manage multiple flows, or design frameworks for others. It also includes an outward arrow indicating teaching/sharing and integrating new elements (like external data or multiple AIs) seamlessly. This layer often has the user monitoring the entire diagram with ease, switching between modes and strategies fluidly.

6. Mirror and Feedback (Reflection Loop): In the diagram, there's a special loop that comes out from the AI's output and circles back to the user's side labeled "Mirror". This represents the Mirror Principle – the idea that the AI's responses reflect your input and thinking. A PromptMaster watches this reflection. For example, if the output is off, the PromptMaster looks at their own prompt to adjust. The Cold Critic Mode is a part of this reflection loop – it's like holding up a magnifying mirror occasionally to inspect flaws in either the AI's output or your approach. Visually, one might depict this as a mirror icon next to an AI output, shining a light back at the user's prompt icon.

7. Ethical and Purposeful Use (Foundation & Boundary): Encircling the entire diagram is a boundary or frame labeled Ethics & Purpose. This reminds that every part of the system operates within the constraints of using AI responsibly. For instance, alignment isn't just about keeping on technical track, but also moral track (not veering into unethical requests). The user's goals themselves sit on a foundation: why are you prompting? The best

outcomes occur when that foundation is solid (your purpose is clear and worthwhile). In the diagram, this could be a base platform labeled with your end goal and values, upon which you (the user icon) stand while interacting. If the conversation threatens to go outside ethical bounds, that outer frame is a hard stop – a PromptMaster will consciously pull back.

Putting it all together: envision a multi-layered, dynamic system. The user engages the AI through an interface, but behind that interface the PromptMaster sees levers (modes), guidelines (alignment rails), loops (iteration and reflection), and an ongoing exchange of control. The Tier progression is like moving from operating one lever at a time to orchestrating the whole control panel, eventually almost automating parts of it through skill. The system diagram underscores that prompt mastery is not a single trick but an interplay of components: user intention, structured prompting, mode management, feedback analysis, and continuous learning, all underpinned by clear purpose and ethics.

By keeping this conceptual map in mind, you can approach any AI interaction and mentally note: Am I setting context (center)? Am I using the control dials (modes)? Where am I on the flow (process)? Are we staying in bounds (alignment)? If something goes wrong, you can locate which part might've faltered – perhaps you forgot to set a mode, or you lost the alignment thread. The diagram is a reminder that all these pieces work together. Master them in unison, and even complex AI tasks become navigable and even intuitive.

Glossary

- Alignment – The process of keeping the AI's responses focused on the user's true goals and intentions. In practice, alignment means the AI is producing relevant, on-topic, and context-appropriate output that matches what the user actually wants or needs. Maintaining alignment often requires the user to reiterate objectives or constraints, especially in multi-turn conversations where the AI might drift. (Discussed in Chapters 2 and 5 as a key element of guiding AI behavior.)

- Anchor / Goal Anchor – A clear statement in a prompt that reasserts the overarching goal or topic you want the AI to focus on. Anchors help to prevent drift by reminding the model what the central purpose is. For example, "Our goal is to improve customer retention, so keep suggestions focused on that." Using anchors throughout a conversation keeps the AI's "attention" locked on what matters. (Technique emphasized in Chapter 5 on system design.)

- Cold Critic Mode – A prompting mode where the AI is instructed to be brutally honest and critical, offering only negative or flaw-focused feedback. In Cold Critic Mode, the AI will point out weaknesses, logical inconsistencies, shallow reasoning, or any other issues without sugar-coating. This mode is used as a tool for rigorous self-audit of ideas or drafts. It's "cold" because it spares no feelings – exactly what you want when you need to find hidden problems. (Introduced in Chapter 3's discussion of modes, used extensively in Chapter 8's case study and the Challenge in Chapter 9.)

- Drift – The tendency of an AI conversation to stray off-topic or deviate from the intended style/tone over time. Drift can occur for many reasons: ambiguous prompts, changes in context, or the model picking up unintended cues. For instance, you may start talking about one problem and the AI gradually veers into a related but irrelevant subject. PromptMasters constantly monitor for drift and correct it by re-aligning the AI (via clarifications, reminders, or anchor prompts). (Explored in Chapter 2 as a core challenge and managed with techniques from Chapter 5.)

• Drift Loop – A feedback loop where the user notices output drift and brings the AI back on track, often repeatedly. For example, the AI goes off on a tangent, the user corrects it ("Let's refocus on X"), and the conversation continues. If drift happens again, the user corrects again. This loop continues until the drift is eliminated. Ideally, a PromptMaster designs interactions to minimize drift loops by being proactive (using anchors, structure), but when they occur, you engage the loop: detect drift, correct course, continue. (Mentioned in Chapter 5 as part of maintaining coherence in long sessions.)

• Interface Illusion – The false but compelling belief that interacting with an AI through a simple chat interface is just like talking to a human or using any ordinary tool. The illusion masks the reality that you are programming a complex model with your prompts. It leads users to underestimate the need for structure or to assume the AI "understands" more than it does. Overcoming the interface illusion is the first step to becoming a PromptMaster – recognizing that behind the friendly text box, there's a vast but blind system awaiting proper instructions. (The central theme of Chapter 1, "The Interface Illusion.")

• Mirror Principle – The concept that the AI's outputs reflect the inputs and guidance provided by the user. In other words, the AI often acts as a mirror of your own clarity, biases, and thought process. If you prompt poorly, the output will likely be poor (reflecting that poor structure back to you). Conversely, examining AI responses can reveal insights about how you asked the question. PromptMasters use this principle to self-diagnose – e.g., if the answer comes out generic, it might mirror a generic question, prompting the user to be more specific next time. The AI can also highlight your blind spots, effectively showing you a reflection of

242

your thinking that you might not see alone. (Explored in Chapter 6, "The Interface as Mirror.")

• Mode / Mode of Operation – A specific style, persona, or approach that the AI can take on when generating responses. Examples of modes: an analytical mode, a storytelling mode, a Socratic-questioning mode, an optimistic brainstorming mode, etc. Modes influence tone and content; for instance, in a "Devil's Advocate" mode the AI will intentionally argue the opposite side of an idea. By setting a mode, the user tells the AI how to respond, not just what to respond about. (Discussed initially in Chapter 2 and employed throughout, especially in Chapter 5's section on Mode Locking.)

• Mode Locking – The technique of explicitly instructing the AI to remain in a chosen mode or persona for the duration of a session or until further notice. It's like setting a character or role and "locking the door" so the AI doesn't slip out of that role. For example, "You are now an impartial scientific reviewer – remain in this role." Mode locking prevents the AI from drifting into a different tone or perspective unexpectedly. It usually involves reinforcing the role at intervals, especially if the AI output starts to diverge. (Covered in Chapter 5 as a crucial method to maintain consistency.)

• Priming – Supplying an AI with contextual information or initial instructions at the start of a conversation (or before a specific question) to influence the output. Priming can include background facts, a scenario setup, the desired format of the answer, or even the role the AI should assume. Essentially, it's feeding the model what it needs to know upfront. A well-primed prompt sets the stage for the AI to respond accurately and relevantly. Without priming, the AI only has the default context and might make incorrect assumptions. (Used throughout the book; Chapter 5's case study and others demonstrate heavy use of priming for better results.)

• Prompt Chain / Chain Prompting – A sequence of prompts used in succession where each prompt builds on the results of the previous one. Instead of asking for a complex result in one go, a prompt chain breaks the task into stages. For example: Prompt 1 – generate ideas; Prompt 2 – evaluate those ideas; Prompt 3 – expand the best idea. Chain prompting leverages the AI's ability to carry context forward and allows the user to steer the process incrementally. It reduces the cognitive load on the AI for each step and leads to more refined outcomes. (Central to the approach in Chapter 5 and exemplified in the case study of Chapter 8.)

• PromptMaster – n. 1. A practitioner who has achieved Tier 4 mastery in prompting AI. Someone who orchestrates AI interactions with a high degree of skill, intention, and adaptability. 2. adj. (as used in "PromptMastery") Pertaining to the approach or techniques associated with master-level prompting. A PromptMaster not only gets excellent results but also understands and controls the underlying dynamics of the AI's behavior. They often help set best practices and are conscious of the ethical implications of AI usage. (The entire book is about becoming this; formally defined in Chapter 4's Tier System and demonstrated especially in Chapters 7–10.)

• PromptMastery – The art and science of effectively communicating with and directing AI systems to achieve desired outcomes. It blends technical knowledge (how the models respond to inputs) with soft skills (clarity of thought, strategic questioning, creativity, critical thinking). PromptMastery implies a level of fluency where structuring prompts, managing context, and iterating towards better answers becomes almost intuitive. It's not just about knowing tricks; it's about a fundamentally different way of approaching problems with AI as a partner. (The term is used throughout the book to describe the overall discipline being taught.)

• PromptMaster Tier System – A structured framework defining four levels of proficiency in prompt crafting: Tier 1 (Prompt Starter), Tier 2 (Prompt Practitioner), Tier 3 (Prompt Architect), Tier 4 (PromptMaster). Each tier corresponds to specific habits, abilities, and mindsets, from basic use through advanced strategic prompting to fluent mastery and leadership. The tier system serves both as a roadmap for personal development and as a way to tailor training or tool usage to someone's current level. (Detailed in Chapter 4 and referenced in appendices for tracking progress.)

- Tier 1: Prompt Starter – The entry level in the Tier System. A user at this tier treats AI at face value, uses simple one-shot prompts, and often experiences inconsistent results without understanding why. Tier 1 users are prone to the Interface Illusion, largely unaware of techniques to control or structure AI output. (See Chapter 4 and Appendix A for characteristics.)

- Tier 2: Prompt Practitioner – The second level in the Tier System. A practitioner who has learned some effective prompting techniques and applies them with some consistency. They get better results than Tier 1 by using structure and a bit of strategy, but mostly in routine situations. They may still have trouble with complex or lengthy interactions and are in the process of building a deeper systematic understanding. (See Chapter 4 and Appendix A.)

- Tier 3: Prompt Architect – The third level. A user who designs and executes multi-step prompt strategies for complex tasks. Tier 3 Prompt Architects think in terms of entire conversations: they plan prompts ahead, lock modes, manage context proactively, and iterate expertly. They often achieve high-quality, reliable outputs even on difficult tasks. The hallmark of Tier 3 is the shift from trial-and-error to methodology – prompting becomes an engineered process. (See Chapter 4 and Appendix A.)

- Tier 4: PromptMaster – The pinnacle level. A master prompter who operates with fluidity and foresight. They not only handle complex sessions with ease, but also innovate new prompting approaches and can teach or lead others in effective AI use. Tier 4s treat AI as an extension of their thinking, seamlessly integrating it into projects. They are also cognizant of the larger picture – such as how to deploy AI solutions in real-world environments and the ethical implications involved. (See Chapter 4 and throughout later chapters for context.)

• Structure (Prompt Structure) – The deliberate organization and formatting of a prompt or series of prompts to impose order on the AI's output. Structure can refer to the way information is presented to the AI (using lists, sections, bullet points in the prompt) and to what is requested in return (asking for numbered points, specific sections, etc.). By providing structure, you guide the AI to produce more coherent, relevant, and complete responses. Structure is the antidote to vagueness – it's at the heart of why a well-phrased prompt yields better results than a careless one. (Emphasized from Chapter 1 onward; "AI responds to structure, not just words" is a recurring theme.)

• (The) Compact – Shorthand in this book for The PromptMaster's Compact, a formal set of guiding principles that capture the philosophy of prompt mastery. It's essentially a "code" summarizing how one should approach AI (e.g., always seek structure, iterate, verify, uphold ethics, etc.). The Compact is meant to be a takeaway reference that distills all the lessons into core commitments. (Presented in Chapter 10 as the capstone of the book.)

• (The) Framework – In context, refers to the overall PromptMaster framework – the entire system of concepts, techniques, and progression put forth in this book. It includes the tier system, the modes, the prompting strategies, and philosophical guidelines. Sometimes "the framework" specifically points to the structural approach for designing AI interactions (as opposed to ad-hoc prompting). It's basically the book's methodology encapsulated. (Mentioned in the Introduction and throughout as what the book is delivering to the reader.)

Index

Mode Locking – detailed in Chapter 5 (technique to pin AI to a mode); utilized in examples in Chapter 8 (maintaining "InsightArchitect" role).

Priming – demonstrated starting in Chapter 1 and Chapter 2 (initial prompt examples) and heavily in Chapter 5 (context priming for system design).

Prompt Chain (Chain Prompting) – strategy highlighted in Chapter 5 (breaking tasks into multi-prompt sequences); the entire Chapter 8 case study is an example of a prompt chain.

PromptMaster (Tier 4 individual) – formally defined in Chapter 4 (Tier System) and exemplified in practice in Chapters 7–10 (advanced integration and leadership in AI use).

PromptMastery – concept introduced in Introduction (what the book is about) and reinforced through every chapter; see especially Chapter 7 (real-
world PromptMastery) and Chapter 10 (principles summarizing PromptMastery).

PromptMaster Tier System – see Chapter 4 for full breakdown of Tier 1–4; Appendix A provides a summary and progress tracker for the tiers.

Tier 1: Prompt Starter – described in Chapter 4 (basic user characteristics) and Appendix A (signs of Tier 1 and how to progress).

Tier 2: Prompt Practitioner – described in Chapter 4 (intermediate user) and Appendix A (traits of Tier 2, moving to Tier 3).

Tier 3: Prompt Architect – described in Chapter 4 (advanced user) and Appendix A (traits of Tier 3, how to reach Tier 4).

Tier 4: PromptMaster – described in Chapter 4 (expert user) and Appendix A (characteristics of Tier 4 mastery).

Structure (Prompt Structure) – emphasized from Chapter 1 (importance of structure) through Chapter 3 and especially in Chapter 5 (designing structured prompt frameworks).

The PromptMaster's Compact – presented in Chapter 10 (list of core principles); serves as an overarching reference to the book's philosophy.

The Framework (PromptMaster framework) – introduced in Introduction ("What This Book Is" section) and implicitly used as a term for the entire approach throughout parts of Chapter 5 and Chapter 7 (when talking about building systems or applying the framework).